English Grammar Handbook for the TOEFL® Test

音読でたたきこむ TOEFL®テスト英文法

TOEFL is a registered trademark of Educational Testing Service (ETS). This publication (or product) is not endorsed or approved by ETS.

生井 健一 著

南雲堂

TOEFL is a registered trademark of Educational Testing Service (ETS).
This publication (or product) is not endorsed or approved by ETS.

はじめに

　この本にあるのは、アメリカの学校英文法の練習問題および解説であり、スタイルは、TOEFLのものを踏襲している。ここで取り上げられている文法項目は、ごく初歩的なものから、洗練された文章を書くのに必要とされるものまで多岐に渡る。特に仕事で英語を使う人、また留学を希望する人などは、どうしても正確な英語を操る能力が要るので、最低でもこの本に紹介されている項目くらいは押さえておきたいものである。よって、問題を解く際には、ただ単にくじを引くような感覚で問題にあたるのではなく、どうしてそうなるのかを良く考え、知らなかったものは理屈を十分理解した上で、繰り返し音読して問題文ごと暗記してしまうことをお勧めする。そして英語を実際に書く（または話す）際に、新しい知識を積極的に使って記憶をより確実なものにしていってほしい。

　さて、文法項目と言っても、実際に使われる重要なものはそれほど多くない。本書では、最近のTOEFLにおける文法セクションに出題された問題のパターンを200に厳選し、前半の100題くらいで主に文法項目の解説を行い、後半では、特に重要と思われる成句および個々の単語の使われ方を紹介した。また、ポイントをわかりやすくするために、各問題文中の単語のレベルはあまり難しくないものに抑えた。しかしながら、TOEFLにおける純粋に文法を問う問題の対策としては、本書の内容でその9割以上をカバーできると言える。後は、単語と成句をどれだけ知っているかの勝負で、これは、リーディング、リスニングのみならず、文法セクションでの高得点にも欠かせない。実用的な英文法など、それほど難しくないので、本書で早くポイントを押さえて、後は単語および成句の知識を増やすことのほうにエネルギーを費やしてほしい。結局のところ、この知識が英語の総合力を決定するのだから。

　I would like to thank Curtis McFarland, Yuri Noma and Kenji Suzuki for proofreading the first draft of this book. I would also like to thank William Rozycki and Kentaro Wakui for their very helpful comments.

生井　健一

本書の使い方

　本書は大きく分けて3つのパートから成っている。パート1が本書の心臓部。10ずつの例題の後に解説がなされている。(訳文は意訳なので、あくまでも参考程度に) 問題は全部で200。答を選ぶ際に「どうしてそうなのか」をきちんと考え、その上で解説にあたってほしい。その後、問題文を繰り返し音読して、できれば文章をすべて暗記してしまおう。(付属のCDはこの目的のためにある。その具体的な使い方は、付属の小冊子参照。) 各文法項目を押さえたこれら200の例文ストックが頭の中にあれば、英作文(および英会話)のときに必ず役に立つ。(特にコンピュータを用いて受験する最近のTOEFL-CBTでは英作文が必須であるので、TOEFL受験を考えている人は英作文対策の第一歩になるであろう。)

　パート2には、パート1の解説に間接的に関連する事項をNotesという形でまとめたものと、各特徴ごとに集められた英単語と表現のリストがある。パート1の解説中でNoteとListについての言及があるときはここを見てほしい。

　パート3は知識の確認のための練習問題集。40題ずつのテスト形式になっていて、テストは全部で5つある。テスト範囲はパート1の例題番号に準拠しているので、パート1で40の例題を終わらせるごとにパート3のテストを1つずつやってみることができる。もちろん、パート1の例題をすべて解いてからパート3のテストを一気にやっても構わない。また、各問題の答には、パート1中のどの例題に準拠する問題であるのかを「☞」で示してあるので、適宜これを利用して解説を読み直し、知識をより確実なものにしていってほしい。

　TOEFLの対策としては、本書の例題および練習問題がそれぞれ約30秒で解けるようになりたい。そのためには練習あるのみ。まず、本書の問題を何度も繰り返し解いてみて、瞬間的に「どういう理由でどの答になるのか」がわかるようになるまで努力してみよう。その後はETSから出ている実際のTOEFLの問題集にあたって数多くの問題を解いてみる。単語力が極端に低い場合を除いて、すぐにコツがつかめるはずである。そうすれば自分が英語を書く(または話す)際にも、自然に文法に注意が向くようになり、確実に英語の総合力増進に役立つはずである。

目次

PART 1

1. 形容詞＋名詞(1) — 12
2. 形容詞＋名詞(2) — 12
3. 形容詞＋名詞(3) — 13
4. 形容詞 vs. 分詞 — 13
5. 副詞(1) — 14
6. 副詞(2) — 14
7. 肯定・否定の同意（Affirmative / Negative Agreement） — 15
8. 一致(1)：時制 — 15
9. 一致(2)：再帰代名詞 — 16
10. 一致(3)：数量詞 — 16
11. 一致(4)：集合名詞 — 20
12. 一致(5)：数量詞主語 — 20
13. 一致(6)：主語・動詞・代名詞 — 21
14. 一致(7)：単複同形名詞 — 21
15. 一致(8)：other — 21
16. 一致(9)：various — 21
17. 一致(10)：不可算名詞 — 22
18. 一致(11)：both — 22
19. 同格 — 22
20. 冠詞(1)：学問分野等 — 23
21. 冠詞(2)：定冠詞 — 26
22. 冠詞(3)：不定冠詞 — 26
23. 可算名詞 vs. 不可算名詞 — 27
24. 格(1)：目的格 — 27
25. 格(2)：所有格 — 27
26. 強調構文 — 28
27. 比較級(1) — 28
28. 比較級(2) — 29
29. 比べるものを同じに(1) — 29
30. 比べるものを同じに(2) — 29
31. 複合名詞 — 32
32. 条件節(1)：仮定法 — 32
33. 条件節(2) — 33
34. 接続詞 — 33
35. 二重目的語 — 33
36. 二重主語 — 34
37. there is / are — 34
38. 動名詞(1) — 34
39. 動名詞(2) — 35
40. 命令文 — 35
41. to 不定詞(1) — 38
42. to 不定詞(2) — 38
43. to 不定詞(3) — 39
44. 助動詞 — 39
45. ～倍(1) — 39
46. ～倍(2) — 40
47. 数字(1) — 40
48. 数字(2) — 41
49. 数字(3) — 41
50. 並列構造(1) — 41
51. 並列構造(2) — 44
52. 並列構造(3) — 44
53. 並列構造(4) — 44
54. 並列構造(5) — 45
55. 分詞構文(1) — 45
56. 分詞構文(2) — 45
57. 分詞構文(3) — 46
58. 分詞構文(4) — 46
59. 分詞構文(5) — 47
60. 分詞の形容詞的用法(1) — 47
61. 分詞の形容詞的用法(2) — 50
62. 分詞の形容詞的用法(3) — 50
63. 受動態(1) — 51
64. 受動態(2) — 51
65. 受動態(3) — 51
66. 後からの修飾句 — 52
67. 前置詞 — 52
68. 現在完了(1) — 53
69. 現在完了(2) — 53
70. 代名詞(1) — 54
71. 代名詞(2) — 58

72. 発音	58	
73. 関係副詞(1)	59	
74. 関係副詞(2)	59	
75. 関係代名詞(1)	59	
76. 関係代名詞(2)	60	
77. 関係代名詞(3)	60	
78. 関係代名詞(4)	60	
79. 関係代名詞(5)	61	
80. 関係代名詞(6)	61	
81. 先行詞を兼ねた関係詞	64	
82. 逆順のパターン(1)	64	
83. 逆順のパターン(2)	65	
84. 逆順のパターン(3)	65	
85. 逆順のパターン(4)	66	
86. 時制(1)	66	
87. 時制(2)	66	
88. 強調の倒置(1)	67	
89. 強調の倒置(2)	67	
90. 命令・要求のときの原形(1)	67	
91. 命令・要求のときの原形(2)	70	
92. 最上級(1)	70	
93. 最上級(2)	70	
94. S＋V(1)	71	
95. S＋V(2)	71	
96. S＋V(3)	71	
97. SVC	72	
98. SVOC(1)	72	
99. SVOC(2)	72	
100. same as	73	
101. same - as	76	
102. keep A from B	76	
103. look forward to	77	
104. (un) like vs. alike	77	
105. 接続詞	77	
106. years of age	78	
107. 副詞 vs. 形容詞	78	
108. in need of	79	
109. a number of, etc.	79	
110. known for	79	
111. a great deal of	82	
112. act on	82	
113. along with	82	
114. already vs. yet	83	
115. any other	83	
116. appear to	83	
117. as - as	84	
118. as in	84	
119. associate A with B	84	
120. begin to	85	
121. benefit from	88	
122. between A and B	88	
123. both A and B	89	
124. by	89	
125. by oneself	90	
126. be concerned about	90	
127. continue to	90	
128. 温度	91	
129. despite / in spite of	91	
130. differ	92	
131. each / every	96	
132. each other	96	
133. neither A nor B	96	
134. enjoy＋動名詞	97	
135. enough	97	
136. first vs. firstly	97	
137. from A to B	97	
138. get - to	98	
139. 間接目的語	98	
140. good vs. well	99	
141. have no idea	102	
142. hear vs. listen	102	
143. help	103	
144. in the world	103	
145. including	103	

146. interested in	104	183. (un)related to	129	
147. know how to	104	184. up vs. upward	129	
148. less	105	185. be / get used to	129	
149. less vs. lesser	105	186. useful for	130	
150. 成句の合作	105	187. wish	130	
151. on the basis of	108	188. with vs. together	131	
152. on time	108	189. would rather (1)	131	
153. one another	108	190. would rather (2)	132	
154. one in …	109	191. such as (1)	136	
155. one of …	109	192. such as (2)	136	
156. one's own	109	193. in response to	137	
157. only a few	110	194. such - that	137	
158. out of …	110	195. take care	137	
159. persuade	110	196. take - by surprise	138	
160. plan to vs. plan on	111	197. 五感の動詞	138	
161. like	114	198. 接続詞 that	138	
162. little	114	199. the ＋名詞	139	
163. located	115	200. the -er, the -er	139	
164. make up for	115			
165. 使役動詞	116	**PART 2**		
166. many	116			
167. much	116	Note 1：Heavy NP-Shift	142	
168. no longer	117	Note 2：倒置	143	
169. not A but B	117	Note 3：another と the other	143	
170. not only A but also B	118	Note 4：関係節の制限的用法・非制限的用法	143	
171. rather than	122			
172. regarding	122	Note 5：句動詞	144	
173. relocate	122	Note 6：形容詞の限定的用法と叙述的用法	145	
174. serve	123			
175. several	123	Note 7：need の使い方	146	
176. should have ＋過去分詞	123	Note 8：concerned	146	
177. show promise of	124	Note 9：文法的に単数である証拠	146	
178. so ~ that	124	Note 10：either / neither	147	
179. so that	124	Note 11：boring と bored	147	
180. spend time	125			
181. the next / coming	128	List 1：単複同形の名詞	148	
182. thousands of	128	List 2：発音で気をつけるもの	148	

List 3：要求・命令の形容詞　　148
List 4：要求・命令の動詞　　　149
List 5：to不定詞をとる動詞　　149
List 6：to不定詞、動名詞ともにとる
　　　　動詞　　　　　　　　150
List 7：動名詞のみをとる動詞　150
List 8：慣例的にtheのつくもの　151

PART 3

Practice Test 1　　　　　154
Practice Test 2　　　　　161
Practice Test 3　　　　　168
Practice Test 4　　　　　175
Practice Test 5　　　　　183

English Grammar Handbook for the TOEFL® Test

PART 1

Directions: Questions 1-10 are incomplete sentences. Beneath each sentence, you will see four words or phrases, marked a, b, c, and d. Choose the **one** word or phrase that best completes the sentence.

1. The Japanese wolf was thought to be a ------- and was hunted to extinction.

    a. danger animal
    b. dangerous animal
    c. animal danger
    d. danger and animal

2. Despite some -------, the National University of Singapore is admitting more foreign students.

    a. locally protests
    b. locally protester
    c. locals and protested
    d. local protests

3. The scientist's ------- was in what she thought to be a simple chemical reaction.

    a. initial interest
    b. initially interesting
    c. initial interesting
    d. interesting initials

4. In the end, we succeeded in making a film out of the science fiction, while still managing to make it feel -------.

    a. believed
    b. believing
    c. believable
    d. like being a believer

5. We should check ------- that there are no careless mistakes before we turn in our exams.

    a. care
    b. careful
    c. carefully
    d. carefulness

6. We would like to offer a ------- more sophisticated cruise experience, from upgraded cuisine to curtains and double beds in the berths.

   a. signifying
   b. signified
   c. significant
   d. significantly

7. During the interview, the author's legs were crossed, and much of the time -------, as if she was shielding herself from public prying.

   a. neither were her arms
   b. her arms did so
   c. so were her arms
   d. her arms didn't either

8. The announcement that scientists have made the first reading of the human genetic code marks the next major step in the project, since scientists ------- decoding the human genome last June.

   a. will have finished
   b. will finish
   c. has finished
   d. finished

9. In his nervous gestures, his discomfort with the situation clearly -------.

   a. manifesting them
   b. has manifested it
   c. will be manifesting by himself
   d. manifested itself

10. ------- of computer program that has been developed at the institute is an excellent machine translation program.

    a. Many sort
    b. A certain kinds
    c. Two variety
    d. One type

解　答	1: b	2: d	3: a	4: c	5: c	6: d	7: c	8: d	9: d	10: d

1. The Japanese wolf was thought to be a ------- and was hunted to extinction.
   a. danger animal
   b. dangerous animal
   c. animal dangers
   d. danger and animal

答：b　ニホンオオカミは危険な動物であると思われ、乱獲の結果絶滅してしまった。

1．形容詞＋名詞⑴

名詞を修飾するのはふつう形容詞である。ここで形容詞＋名詞（dangerous＋animal）の形をなしているのはbだけ。

2. Despite some -------, the National University of Singapore is admitting more foreign students.
   a. locally protests
   b. locally protester
   c. locals and protested
   d. local protests

答：d　地元に抗議があるにも関わらず、シンガポール国立大学は外国人学生の数を増やしている。

2．形容詞＋名詞⑵

形容詞と副詞の使い方をみる問題。a、bともに副詞＋名詞であるのでアウト。（副詞は名詞以外の品詞を修飾するが、このことが出題されることもある）。cは名詞のlocalsと動詞のprotestedがandで結ばれていて意味をなさない（問題50〜54の並列構造参照）。形容詞のlocalが名詞protestsを修飾するdのみが正しい形である。

3. The scientist's ------- was in what she thought to be a simple chemical reaction.
   a. initial interest
   b. initially interesting
   c. initial interesting
   d. interesting initials

答：a　簡単な化学反応にすぎないと思っていたものに科学者は最初興味を持っていた。

3．形容詞＋名詞(3)
　答の入る部分はwasの直前なので主語である。The scientist's「科学者の」ときているから、名詞句が要求されていることがわかる。bは副詞＋形容詞、cは形容詞＋形容詞であるからともに候補から消える。dは形容詞＋名詞ではあるが、その意味「興味深いイニシャル」が文意に合わず、その上、initialsとwasでは数の一致が見られない。よって答はa。

---

4. In the end, we succeeded in making a film out of the science fiction, while still managing to make it feel -------.
   a. believed
   b. believing
   c. believable
   d. like being a believer

答：c　我々は最終的にそのSFからいかにもありそうな話の映画を作り出すことに成功した。

4．形容詞vs.分詞
　単語の意味の問題。while以下は「それ（＝映画）をどうにかbelievableに感じさせながら」というもの。映画が「信じられる」、つまりその内容が「ありえそうだ」という「可能」の意味が一番しっくりくる。aの過去分詞「信じられる（受身）」、bの現在分詞「信じる、信じている」は、ここではおかしい。dのfeel like -ingは「～したい」という意味なのでアウトである（feel＋形容詞のパターンについては、問題197参照）。

---

5. We should check ------- that there are no careless mistakes before we turn in our exams.
   a. care
   b. careful
   c. carefully
   d. carefulness

答：c　試験を提出する前に、ケアレスミスがないように注意深くチェックするべきだ。

5．副詞(1)

　副詞が動詞を修飾するパターン。意味の上から「注意深く」は動詞checkにかかる。よって副詞carefullyが答である。ここで注意したいのは、carefullyの位置。ふつうはcheck A carefully「Aを注意深くチェックする」のように目的語の後に置かれるのだが、問題文にあるように目的語にあたる部分（ここではthat節）が長い場合、文の座りをよくするため、また、carefullyが従属節内の動詞でなく、主節にある動詞（ここではcheck）を修飾することをはっきりさせるために、目的語を文末に移動させて表面上check carefully Aという語順になることがある（Heavy-NP Shift: Note 1参照）。あくまでも目的語が長い場合だけに起こる現象なので、目的語が短い場合には適用しないように。

---

6. We would like to offer a ------- more sophisticated cruise experience, from upgraded cuisine to curtains and double beds in the berths.
   a. signifying
   b. signified
   c. significant
   d. significantly

答：d　ワンランク上の食事から寝台室のカーテンとダブルベッドに至るまで、はるかに洗練されたクルーズ体験を提供したいと思っております。

6．副詞(2)

　副詞が形容詞（分詞の形容詞的用法を含む）を修飾するパターン。ここではmore sophisticated「より洗練された」という形容詞の比較級を修飾するので、副詞significantlyが答となる。(他の選択肢はいずれも形容詞を修飾できない。)

---

7. During the interview, the author's legs were crossed, and much of the time -------, as if she was shielding herself from public prying.
   a. neither were her arms
   b. her arms did so
   c. so were her arms
   d. her arms didn't either

答：c　インタビューの間作家は足を組み、しょっちゅう腕組みもして、あたかも公衆の詮索から自らを守っているようだった。

7．肯定・否定の同意（Affirmative / Negative Agreement）
　「～も」は、肯定のときは too、否定のときは either を文末につけることによって表されるが、so と neither を文頭に置いてもよい。ただし、この場合主語と助動詞（あるいは be 動詞）の倒置が起こるので注意。ここでは the author's legs were crossed に対して、「腕も組まれていた」というのをどう表現するのかが問題になっている。肯定文なので a と d が消える。また、b の did は were であるべき。その上、最後に too でなく so が来ているのでアウト。c の so were her arms のみが so＋倒置のルールにのっとっている（問題88、89および Note 2 参照）。

---

8. The announcement that scientists have made the first reading of the human genetic code marks the next major step in the project, since scientists ------- decoding the human genome last June.
   a. will have finished
   b. will finish
   c. has finished
   d. finished

答：d　科学者がヒトの遺伝子コードの最初の読み取りに成功したという発表は、プロジェクトにおける次の大きなステップを印すものである。というのも、去年の6月に科学者はヒトゲノムの解析を終わらせているからだ。

8．一致(1)：時制
　文末にある last June は明らかに過去の表現。よって求められている動詞も過去形でなければならない。a、b はともに未来、c は現在完了なので last June とともに用いられることはない（問題69参照）。答は d。

---

9. In his nervous gestures, his discomfort with the situation clearly -------.
   a. manifesting them
   b. has manifested it
   c. will be manifesting by himself
   d. manifested itself

答：d　その状況が不快であることは、彼のいらいらしたジェスチャーにはっきり表れていた。

9．一致(2)：再帰代名詞
　ここでのmanifestは「～を表す」という他動詞。よって目的語が必要となるが、cにはそれがないし、by himself「自分自身で」という表現が意味の上でおかしい。aではthemの指すものの問題のほか、動詞が正しい形になっていない。進行形としてもbe動詞がないからだ。bにおいてはitの指すものがない。もし主語のhis discomfort with the situationを指すのなら、itselfでないとまずい。これは、SVOの構文で、S＝Oであるなら、Oは再帰代名詞（-self）になるという代名詞のルールに基づくもの。e.g. He loves himself.「彼は自分自身を愛している。」よって、答はd。manifest oneselfのパターンはよく見られるので、セットにして覚えておいてもよい。

> 10. ------- of computer program that has been developed at the institute is an excellent machine translation program.
>   a. Many sort
>   b. A certain kinds
>   c. Two variety
>   d. One type
>
> 答：d　その研究所で開発されたコンピュータ・プログラムの1つのタイプは優秀な機械翻訳プログラムである。

10．一致(3)：数量詞
　「種類」を表す名詞とそれに伴う冠詞や数量詞との間における数の一致に関する問題。aではmany（複数）とsort（単数）、bではa certain（単数）とkinds（複数）、cではtwo（複数）とvariety（単数）というように、いずれも数の一致が見られない。よって答は単数で統一されているd。ちなみにa variety of ...には「多くの…」と「…の一種」という2つの意味がある。前者の場合「…」に入る名詞は必ず複数、後者では単数でもOKだが無冠詞になることを覚えておこう。

Directions: In questions 11-20 each sentence has four underlined words or phrases. The four underlined parts of the sentence are marked a, b, c, and d. Identify the **one** underlined word or phrase that must be changed in order for the sentence to be correct.

11. I love these three collection of folk songs produced by Ken Marcus in
            a   b   c   d
    the 1970's.

12. At least three out of every four Ph.D. students at that university fails
      a   b   c   d
    to graduate.

13. Unlike most of his colleagues, the biology professors still appears to
       a   b   c
    be in good health.
        d

14. Native to Southeast Asia, those species of lizard is found in wet
        a   b   c   d
    regions.

15. In the Department of Physics, as in other department at the university,
                                  a   b   c
    students are expected to write a graduation thesis
    of a publishable quality.
          d

16. They were unable to attend the meeting for various reason.
          a   b   c   d

17. Her knowledge of three languages and economics help her greatly in
              a   b   c   d
    her work.

18. Before you call it a day, you must paint both side of this wall.
       a   b   c d

19. One of the typical metropolitan cities often used in market research is
                                    ‾‾‾‾‾ ‾‾‾‾‾‾‾‾‾‾ ‾‾‾‾‾‾‾‾‾‾‾‾‾‾‾‾‾‾
                                      a   b   c
    Columbus, Ohio, of the capital of the state.
                    ‾‾‾‾‾‾‾‾‾‾‾‾‾‾‾
                          d

20. The forensic linguistics is a relatively new field, but it has already
    ‾‾‾‾‾‾‾‾‾‾‾‾‾‾‾‾‾‾‾‾‾‾‾‾   ‾‾‾‾‾‾‾‾‾‾
                a   b
    attracted many researchers because of its promising future.
    ‾‾‾‾‾‾‾‾‾   ‾‾‾‾‾‾‾‾‾
        c   d

| 解　答 | 11: b | 12: d | 13: c | 14: b | 15: b | 16: d | 17: b | 18: c | 19: d | 20: a |

11. I love <u>these</u> three <u>collection</u> of <u>folk songs</u> produced by Ken Marcus <u>in the</u>
　　　　　a　　　　　　b　　　　　　　c　　　　　　　　　　　　　　　　　　　d
1970's.

答：b（collection → collections）僕は1970年代にケン・マーカスによってプロデュースされたこれら3つのフォークソング・コレクションが大好きだ。

11.　一致(4)：集合名詞

　数量詞と collection, team, class のような集合名詞との間の一致の問題。集合名詞も結局ふつうの可算名詞なので複数である場合 -s がつく。問題文ではフォークソングのコレクション（つまりアルバム）が3つと言っているので、three collections となるべき。

12. <u>At least three</u> out of <u>every four Ph.D. students</u> <u>at that university</u> <u>fails to</u>
　　　　　a　　　　　　　　　　　b　　　　　　　　　　　　c　　　　　　　　　　d
graduate.

答：d（fails → fail）その大学では、少なくとも4人に3人の博士課程の学生が卒業できない。

12.　一致(5)：数量詞主語

　主語・動詞間における一致の問題。この文の主語はとても長いが、単複を決定する主要部は three である。これはもちろん複数なので、動詞も fails ではなく fail が正しい。every という語は文法的には単数であるという事実（問題131参照）に惑わされないように。（ここでは4人の博士課程の学生を1つの単位とみなしているので every と students が共起している。このような表現は以下のようなものにも見られる。e.g. once every three days「3日（ごと）に1度」。）

13. <u>Unlike</u> most of <u>his colleagues</u>, <u>the biology professors</u> still appears to be
　　　　a　　　　　　　　b　　　　　　　　　　　　　c
<u>in good health</u>.
　　　d

答：c（the biology professors → the biology professor）生物学教授は、彼の同僚のほとんどとは違い、まだ健康そうである。

13. 一致(6)：主語・動詞・代名詞

これも主語・動詞間の一致の問題。主語の the biology professors の複数に合わせて b の his を their にしたとしても、動詞が appears なので問題は解決されない。しかし、主語を単数にすれば b を直すことなく主語・動詞間の一致（三単現の-s）を確立することができる。

14. Native to Southeast Asia, those species of lizard is found in wet regions.
　　　　　　　　　　　　　　　a　　　b　　c　　　　d

答：b（those → that）東南アジアに特有であるそのトカゲの種は、湿地帯に見られる。

14. 一致(7)：単複同形名詞

指示詞と名詞の一致の問題。まず主語をなす those species of lizard 中で species が主語・動詞間の一致を決定する主要部であることを見抜く。species は単複同形なので those species 自体には問題ないが、動詞が単数の is なのでこの文中の species は単数であることがわかる。よって、それを修飾する指示詞が複数の those ではおかしいことになる（List 1 参照）。

15. In the Department of Physics, as in other department at the university,
　　　　　　　　　　　　　　　　　　a　　　　b　　　　c
　　students are expected to write a graduation thesis of a publishable quality.
　　　　　　　　　　　　　　　　　　　　　　　　　　　　d

答：b（department → departments）その大学の他学科同様物理学科でも、学会誌に載るくらいの卒論を書くことが学生に求められている。

15. 一致(8)：other

other とそれに後続する名詞における数の一致の問題。other は複数なので、名詞のほうも常に複数。ただし定冠詞を伴い、the other となるとこの限りではなく、文脈によっては単数名詞が来る場合がある（Note 3 参照）。

16. They were unable to attend the meeting for various reason.
　　　　　　　　a　　　　　b　　　　　　　　c　　　　d

答：d（reason → reasons）彼らはさまざまな理由でミーティングに出席できなかった。

16. 一致(9)：various

前問の other 同様、various も常に複数名詞をとる。「さまざまな」という意味からしても当然であろう。

17. Her knowledge of three languages and economics help her greatly in her work.
　　　　　　　　　a　　　　　　　　　　　　　　　　　　　 b　　　 c　　　　d

答：b (help → helps)　3ヶ国語と経済学を知っていることが、仕事において彼女の大きな助けになっている。

17．一致(10)：不可算名詞

　動詞の直前にthree languages and economicsという複数の名詞句があるが、主語の主要部は不可算名詞（常に単数扱い）のknowledge。よって動詞には三単現の-sが必要（あるいは過去形のhelpedでもよい）。これも主語・動詞間の一致の問題。

---

18. Before you call it a day, you must paint both side of this wall.
　　　　　　 a　　　　 b　　　　　　　　　　　　　　 c　　 d

答：c (side → sides)　仕事を終える前に、この壁の両面を塗らないといけないよ。

18．一致(11)：both

　both「両方」もその意味から常に複数なので、後続する名詞も複数。もちろんA and Bの形が来れば、A、Bともに単数ということもあるが、結局A and B全体で複数になっている。(call it a day = finish working for the day)

---

19. One of the typical metropolitan cities often used in market research is
　　　　　　　　　　　　　　　　　　　 a　　　　 b　　　　　　　　 c
　　Columbus, Ohio, of the capital of the state.
　　　　　　　　　　　　 d

答：d (of the capital → the capital)　市場調査によく使われる典型的な大都市の1つがオハイオ州の州都コロンバスである。

19．同格

　まず、この文はColumbus, Ohioで終えてしまっても完結した文になることに注目。オハイオ州のコロンバスがどういう都市なのかを説明するのにd以下が加えられている。こういう目的のためには関係代名詞がよく使われるが、確かにd which is the capitalとしてもよい。しかし、こなれた文中によく見られるのは同格の形、つまりColumbus, Ohio, the capital of the state「コロンバス・オハイオ、その州の州都」というもの。TOEFLでも頻出のパターンである。問題文にあるようにofでつなごうとすると意味をなさない文ができてしまう。

20. The forensic linguistics is a relatively new field, but it has already attracted
    ─────────────────────   ─ ────────   ─────────
              a   b   c
    many researchers because of its promising future.
                                    ─────────
                                        d

答：a（The forensic linguistics → Forensic linguistics）犯罪言語学は比較的新しい分野であるが、発展の見込みがあるためすでに多くの研究者が生まれている。

20．冠詞⑴：学問分野等

通例学問分野等（biology、history、mathematics、science、etc.）の名前は無冠詞で使われる。ここでも特定のものではなく犯罪言語学一般について言っているのだから無冠詞であるべき。

Directions: Questions 21-30 are incomplete sentences. Beneath each sentence, you will see four words or phrases, marked a, b, c, and d. Choose the **one** word or phrase that best completes the sentence.

21. Dr. Noguchi tried to find the cause of yellow fever in the early 20th century, in ------- the advent of the electron microscope.

    a. a preceding decades
    b. the decades preceding
    c. decades followed by
    d. a following decade

22. His reports are always dubious, because he never gets information from any reliable source but instead from ------- obscure secondary source.

    a. more significant
    b. those more
    c. considerably more
    d. a much more

23. The Peterson Home for ------- is one of the best reform schools in the nation.

    a. Aged Woman
    b. Elderly Man
    c. Child and Baby
    d. Boys

24. The musicians suggested that the scores be sent to ------- by special delivery so that they could get to work on the project immediately.

    a. they
    b. their
    c. them
    d. theirs

25. Although Miss White gave a definitive answer, her students looked for ------- own creative solutions.

    a. they
    b. their
    c. them
    d. theirs

26. Karen is a very warm person, and ------- is that aspect of her character that has enabled her to get her friends to trust her with intimate stories about their lives.

    a. both
    b. which
    c. and
    d. it

27. Carbon dioxide and other greenhouse gases from human activities are ------- the one-degree rise in global temperature since 1950 than most other possible causes.

    a. more likely to have caused
    b. likely to be the cause of
    c. very much likely to have caused
    d. to be blamed for the likely cause of

28. Many people expect the economy to be better off in six months ------- .

    a. after the economy of tomorrow will be
    b. of all the months ahead of them
    c. as today
    d. than it is today

29. Last week's economics lecture was a comparison of the economy today and ------- , the last time the United States suffered a recession.

    a. the year of 1990
    b. that of 1990
    c. the past year of 1990
    d. the 1990 of the economy

30. Despite the general slowdown, which dragged down its shares more than ------- , the computer company has managed to strongly outsell many of them.

    a. its rivals
    b. most of the rivals
    c. those of most of its rivals
    d. those rivals they fear

| 解 答 | 21: b | 22: d | 23: d | 24: c | 25: b | 26: d | 27: a | 28: d | 29: b | 30: c |

21. Dr. Noguchi tried to find the cause of yellow fever in the early 20th century, in ------- the advent of the electron microscope.
   a. a preceding decades
   b. the decades preceding
   c. decades followed by
   d. a following decade

答：b 野口博士は20世紀の初頭、電子顕微鏡が出現する前の時代に、黄熱病の原因を見つけようとした。

21．冠詞(2)：定冠詞

in the early 20th century と in the decades preceding the advent of the electron microscope がカンマを介し同格として並んでいる。問題19同様、後者が前者の説明になっているパターン。20世紀初頭と期間を限定しているので、decades「数十年」には定冠詞のthe が必要である。よってthe がついているbのみが答。

22. His reports are always dubious, because he never gets information from any reliable source but instead from ------- obscure secondary source.
   a. more significant
   b. those more
   c. considerably more
   d. a much more

答：d 彼のレポートはいつも疑わしい。というのも、彼は決して信頼できる筋からではなく、代わりにずっと怪しい二流の筋から情報を得ているからだ。

22．冠詞(3)：不定冠詞

source という名詞は可算名詞である。よって複数形でない限り、冠詞が必要となる。前半にある reliable source には any がついているので問題ない（some と any は単数名詞につくこともある）。後半の obscure secondary source は複数形でないので不定冠詞のa が必要。選択肢a と c には何も冠詞がないし、bの指示詞those は複数なのでアウト。よって答は d。

23. The Peterson Home for ------- is one of the best reform schools in the nation.
   a. Aged Woman
   b. Elderly Man
   c. Child and Baby
   d. Boys

答：d ピーターソン・ホーム・フォー・ボーイズは国中で最も優秀な少年院の1つである。

23. 可算名詞 vs. 不可算名詞

選択肢にある名詞はすべて可算名詞である。よってふつう単数形で使われる場合は不定冠詞のaが必要になる。しかし、a、b、cにおいてはこのルールが守られていないのでアウト。よってdのBoysが答となるが、ここでは意味の上からも複数形がぴったりであろう。

---

24. The musicians suggested that the scores be sent to ------- by special delivery so that they could get to work on the project immediately.
    a. they
    b. their
    c. them
    d. theirs

答：c 音楽家たちは直ちにそのプロジェクトに取り掛かれるよう、楽譜を速達で受け取ることを主張した。

---

24. 格(1)：目的格

代名詞の格の問題。ここでは前置詞 to に後続する代名詞の形が問題になっている。「前置詞のあとは目的格」と覚えておけばよい。d の theirs「彼らのもの」は主格にも目的格にもなるが、この場合意味の上ではじかれる。スコアが送られるのは them = the musicians にであり theirs「彼らのもの」にではないからだ。

---

25. Although Miss White gave a definitive answer, her students looked for ------- own creative solutions.
    a. they
    b. their
    c. them
    d. theirs

答：b ホワイト先生は最終的な答を教えたが、生徒たちは自分たちの創造的な解決策を探すことにした。

---

25. 格(2)：所有格

own に注目。「〜自身の」という意味の own は常に所有格とともに用いられる。よって答は b。

26. Karen is a very warm person, and ------- is that aspect of her character that has enabled her to get her friends to trust her with intimate stories about their lives.
   a. both
   b. which
   c. and
   d. it

答：d　カレンはとても心が温かく、彼女の友達が自分たちの生活における個人的な話まで彼女にしてしまうのは、彼女のそういうところによるものである。

26．強調構文
　　強調されている名詞句 that aspect of her character「彼女のキャラクターのその側面（つまり、彼女が心温かい人であること）」に that があってややこしく見えるが、it is A that B「B であるのは A」という強調構文なので答は d。

27. Carbon dioxide and other greenhouse gases from human activities are ------- the one-degree rise in global temperature since 1950 than most other possible causes.
   a. more likely to have caused
   b. likely to be the cause of
   c. very much likely to have caused
   d. to be blamed for the likely cause of

答：a　1950年以来地球気温が1度上昇したのは、人々の営みから出される二酸化炭素とその他の温室効果を持つ気体が原因で、他に考えられる理由のほとんどのせいではなさそうだ。

27．比較級(1)
　　ややこしく見える問題であるが1950の後に than があることに気がつけば後は簡単。つまり比較級を要求しているのである。選択肢の中で比較級があるのは a だけ。more が than とセットになって比較文を構成する。

28. Many people expect the economy to be better off in six months -------.
   a. after the economy of tomorrow will be
   b. of all the months ahead of them
   c. as today
   d. than it is today

答：d　景気は6ヶ月後には現在よりよくなっているだろうと、多くの人が思っている。

28. 比較級(2)

問題27と逆のパターン。問題文に比較級betterがあるので、それに対応するthanを選べばよい。よって答はd。しかしながら、文脈によってthan以下が省略されることもあるので、一応他の選択肢も見たほうがよいが、ここでは、d以外のどれもめちゃくちゃである。

---

29. Last week's economics lecture was a comparison of the economy today and -------, the last time the United States suffered a recession.
　　a. the year of 1990
　　b. that of 1990
　　c. the past year of 1990
　　d. the 1990 of the economy

答：b　先週の経済学の講義は、今日の景気と1990年、つまりアメリカが最後に不況を経験した年のそれとの比較であった。

---

29. 比べるものを同じに(1)

問題文中の講義が比較したのは、今日の景気と1990年の景気である。本来the economy of 1990とすればよいのだが、英語は繰り返しを嫌うのでthe economyをthatで置き換え、that of 1990とする。すなわちbが答。aのようなものを選ぶと、今日の景気と1990年という年を比べることになりロジカルでなくなるので注意。

---

30. Despite the general slowdown, which dragged down its shares more than -------, the computer company has managed to strongly outsell many of them.
　　a. its rivals
　　b. most of the rivals
　　c. those of most of its rivals
　　d. those rivals they fear

答：c　そのコンピュータ会社は、全般的な景気後退でほとんどのライバル会社よりも株価を下げたが、売上では大きく差をつけた。

---

30. 比べるものを同じに(2)

2つのカンマにはさまれた部分のみが問題になっている。whichが指すのは「(景気の)後退」で、これが話題になっているコンピュータ会社の株を、ほとんどのライバル会社の株よりも引きずりおろした、というのである。ここでも比べられているものはshares「株」であり、「ほとんどのライバル会社の株」はthe shares of most of its rivalsであるべき。よって、繰り返しを避ける代用表現を使うのだが、今回はsharesが複数なので、thatではなくthoseを使う。答はc。

Directions: In questions 31-40 each sentence has four underlined words or phrases. The four underlined parts of the sentence are marked a, b, c, and d. Identify the **one** underlined word or phrase that must be changed in order for the sentence to be correct.

31. As we all know, automobile insure is cheaper in America than
       a b   c
    in Japan.
       d

32. If I were a college student, I will study very hard and try to gain
                                    a   b   c
    as much knowledge as possible.
                d

33. We will surely reach a decision in the next meeting if the incompetent
              a   b
    chairperson will not show up.
             c   d

34. This information might prove useful in the need ever arises to sue
                             a   b   c d
    that incompetent lawyer.

35. The citizens of that country do not even appreciate it their freedom,
               a   b   c
    which they simply take for granted.
                d

36. The visiting English professor from a very prestigious university in
                                    a
    America he told us to watch as many English programs as possible
              b   c
    on satellite TV in order to improve listening comprehension.
     d

37. There has had a decrease in the importation of foreign cars.
          a b   c   d

38. The English teacher complimented one of her students for knowledge
                                                                    a
   more English words than she herself did.
   ‾‾‾‾‾‾‾‾‾‾‾‾‾‾‾‾‾ ‾‾‾‾ ‾‾‾‾‾‾‾‾‾‾‾
           b   c   d

39. During the 1980's, to teach biology at the university was much more
          ‾‾‾   ‾‾‾‾‾‾‾‾   ‾‾
           a   b   c
   effective than it is now.
   ‾‾‾‾‾‾‾‾‾‾‾‾‾‾‾‾‾‾‾‾‾
              d

40. With regard to the possibility of transferring to another school, first
   ‾‾‾‾‾‾‾‾‾‾‾‾‾‾‾   ‾‾‾‾‾‾‾‾‾‾‾‾‾ ‾‾‾‾‾
          a   b   c
   consultation the international student advisor.
   ‾‾‾‾‾‾‾‾‾‾‾
        d

解　答　31. c　32. a　33. c　34. b　35. c　36. b　37. a　38. a　39. b　40. d

---

31. As we all know, automobile insure is cheaper in America than in Japan.
　　　a　　b　　　　　　　　c　　　　　　　　　　　　　　d

答：c（insure → insurance）我々みんなが知っているように、自動車保険は日本よりアメリカのほうが安い。

31．複合名詞

問題文の通りであると、動詞insure「保証する、保険にかける」が主語になってしまう。ふつう、主語になれるのは名詞だけなので、これはinsuranceに直すべき。すると前にある名詞automobileと一緒になってautomobile insurance「自動車保険」という複合名詞ができ、正しい文ができあがる。この例では、automobileが形容詞のようにinsuranceを修飾しているが、形容詞的に用いられる名詞は（一部の例外を除いて）常に単数形であり、これが複合名詞構成の基本になっている。

---

32. If I were a college student, I will study very hard and try to gain
　　　　　　　　　　　　　　　　　　a　　　　　　b　　　　　　c
　　as much knowledge as possible.
　　　　　　　　d

答：a（will study → would study）もし僕が大学生だったら、一生懸命勉強してできる限りの知識を得ようとするのに。

32．条件節(1)：仮定法

現状とは違ったことを仮定して条件付けを行い、「もし～だったら、…するのに」という言い方を問う問題。仮定法過去を使う。この場合、動詞はすべて過去形になるが、意味は「現在」であることに注意。問題文では、条件節が仮定法過去になっているのに、主節の動詞が過去になっていない。よってこれを過去形にすればよい。ちなみに仮定法過去の場合、be動詞は人称に関わらずwereにするのが正しいとされている。また、「もし～だったら、…したのに」（つまり「～でなかったので、…しなかった」というのが事実）というように、過去に起こってしまったことを仮定して言う場合には、仮定法過去完了を使う。条件節はhad＋過去分詞、主節は助動詞の過去形＋have＋過去分詞という形をとる。e.g. If I had known him, I would have talked to him.「もし彼のことを知っていたら、彼に話しかけたのに」（つまり、知らなかったので、話しかけなかったということ）。

---

33. We will surely reach a decision in the next meeting if the incompetent
　　　　　　　　　a　　　　　b
　　chairperson will not show up.
　　　　　　　　c　　　　d

答：c（will not → does not）もし無能な議長が来なければ、我々は次のミーティングできっと何らかの決定を見るだろう。

33. 条件節(2)

「次のミーティング」の話をしているのだから、これは未来の文である。また、仮定法を使っていないので、純粋な条件文ということになる。つまり、議長が来ないという可能性に対してニュートラルな態度が表されている。(仮定法過去を使うと、「議長は必ず来るが、もし来なければ…」というように、「議長が来ない」ことは現実にはあり得ないという含みが出て来る。) さて、本題に入るが、条件節はみな副詞節である。副詞節では、いくら未来のことを言っていても (特別な例外を除いて) will は使わず、現在形を使うルールになっている。よって will not を does not にすればよい。(これは仮定法過去にも適応されるルールで、問題文を仮定法で書くと、We would reach a decision in the next meeting if the incompetent chairperson did not show up になり、would not でないことに注意。) なお、このルールは、主節および名詞節には当てはまらない。

---

34. This information might <u>prove useful</u> in the need <u>ever arises</u> to sue that
　　　　　　　　　　　　　　 a　　　 b　　　　　　c　　　d
incompetent lawyer.

答：b (in → if) 万一あの無能な弁護士を訴えることになったら、この情報は役に立つかもしれない。

---

34. 接続詞

問題文中の in は前置詞なので、後に来るのは名詞句がふつう。ここでは節が来ているので接続詞が必要となり、この情報だけで b を選ぶことができる。in を if に換えれば意味の通る文ができあがる。

---

35. The citizens <u>of</u> that country do <u>not even</u> <u>appreciate it their freedom</u>, which
　　　　　　　　 a　　　　　　　　　　　 b　　　　　　　　 c
they simply <u>take</u> for granted.
　　　　　　　　 d

答：c (appreciate it their freedom → appreciate their freedom) あの国の人たちは、自由を単に当たり前のものとみなし、自由であることをありがたいとさえ思っていない。

---

35. 二重目的語

appreciate「〜をありがたく思う、感謝する」は目的語を1つだけ取る他動詞。それなのに、問題文では it と their freedom の2つが目的語の位置に来ている。代名詞 it が余分なので、それを取り除けばよい。I'd appreciate it.「感謝します」という決り文句に引っ掛けた問題。

36. The visiting English professor from a very prestigious university in America
                                          ─a─
    he told us to watch as many English programs as possible on satellite TV in
    ─b──   ─────────c─────────────   ──d─
    order to improve listening comprehension.

答：b （he told → told） アメリカの超名門大学から来た英文学の客員教授は、リスニング力を増すために、衛星放送でできるだけ多くの英語番組を見なさいと私たちに言った。

36. 二重主語

　この問題文では、The visiting English professor from a very prestigious university in America が主語であるのに、改めて he を主語にして文を始めている。もちろんこれは誤りで、he を消去する必要がある。このパターン（主語を言った後に短いポーズを置き、それを代名詞で受けて文を完成させる）は、会話ではよく見られるが、書き言葉では冗長になるので避けられる。

37. There has had a decrease in the importation of foreign cars.
              ─a─ ─b─   ──c──   ───d────
答：a （had → been） 外国車の輸入に減少が生じた。

37. there is/are

　「〜がある」というときに使われる there は、ふつう be 動詞と共起する。問題文ではそれが現在完了になっているだけである。中学英語の知識だが、ここに再確認しておこう。

38. The English teacher complimented one of her students for knowledge more
                                                              ─────a──── ─b─
    English words than she herself did.
    ──────b───── ──c── ─────d──────
答：a （knowledge → knowing） 英語教員は、自分より多くの英単語を知っていたので、教え子の一人を誉めた。

38. 動名詞(1)

　前置詞の後は名詞句あるいは動名詞が来るのだが、この問題では more English words が knowledge の目的語の位置にあるので、純粋に名詞である knowledge ではなく動名詞の knowing が答になる。つまり、名詞は目的語を取れないが（他動詞の）動名詞は取ることができるということ。

39. During the 1980's, to teach biology at the university was much more effective
         ‾‾a‾‾   ‾‾‾b‾‾‾   ‾‾c‾‾
than it is now.
‾‾‾‾d‾‾‾‾

答：b（to teach → the teaching of）1980年代の間、その大学での生物学教育は今よりもずっと効果的であった。

39．動名詞(2)

　「生物学を教えること」という名詞句は to teach biology（to不定詞）でも teaching biology（動名詞）でもよいのだが、これらには一般論的な意味しかない。「その大学での生物学の教育」というように限定的な意味を出したい場合は、定冠詞 the を用いることになるのだが、to不定詞は the を取らない。そこで、動名詞を名詞とみなして、the teaching of biology とする（名詞なので目的語を直接取ることはできず of を介してつなぐ）。問題２０で見たような学問の名称などでも同じことが言える。e.g. history「歴史」、the history of Japan「日本の歴史」。

40. With regard to the possibility of transferring to another school, first
    ‾‾‾‾‾‾a‾‾‾‾‾‾   ‾‾‾‾b‾‾‾‾‾‾ ‾c‾
consultation the international student advisor.
‾‾‾‾d‾‾‾‾‾

答：d（consultation → consult）転校の可能性については、まずインターナショナル・スチューデント・アドバイザーに相談しなさい。

40．命令文

　この文には主語がないことに目をつけよう。そうすれば命令文であることがすぐわかる。命令文は、動詞の原形を使うので consultation（名詞）を consult（動詞の原形）にすればよい。また、consult、consult with ともに「相談する」と訳されるが、前者は「専門家に助言を求める」、後者は「対等の人と話し合う」という場合に使われる。

Directions: Questions 41-50 are incomplete sentences. Beneath each sentence, you will see four words or phrases, marked a, b, c, and d. Choose the **one** word or phrase that best completes the sentence.

41. Go over your answers as many times as possible ------- that you don't make any careless mistakes.

    a. to making sure
    b. to make sure
    c. to made sure of
    d. make sure of

42. Freddie Mercury's reputation as a great rock singer rests on his ability ------- emotional depth to his songs.

    a. be giving
    b. is giving
    c. being given
    d. to give

43. The State Department urged American citizens ------- to that country, warning that unrest and violence could break out at any time.

    a. not travel
    b. never traveling
    c. not to travel
    d. to not to travel

44. I know students are supposed to study hard, but I don't think we ------- necessarily force them to do so.

    a. had
    b. should
    c. used
    d. have

45. Scientists had expected to find about 100,000 genes per person; instead, they found about 30,000—only ------- a fly has, and 10,000 more than a worm.

    a. three times more
    b. the same number of
    c. a little over
    d. twice as many as

46. When we talk to someone on the telephone, we tend to concentrate ------- on the conversation.

   a. twice as hard
   b. as seriously as
   c. more severely than
   d. the most vigorous of

47. The number of air travelers in the nation climbed nearly 10 percent between 1995 and 2000 to ------- .

   a. 200th million
   b. 200 millions
   c. the 200 millionth
   d. 200 million

48. Flight 852 for San Francisco is now boarding at ------- .

   a. the Gate Five
   b. Fifth Gate
   c. Gate Five
   d. the Gate Fifth

49. I have an appointment to see the professor on ------- of the month.

   a. the first
   b. one
   c. one date
   d. first date

50. Dorothy Stratten was a young, beautiful, and ------- model when she was killed at the age of 20.

   a. talented
   b. had a lot of talent and a skillful
   c. everybody liked her as a
   d. whose talent was of a

解答 41: b　42: d　43: c　44: b　45: d　46: a　47: d　48: c　49: a　50: a

41. Go over your answers as many times as possible ------- that you don't make any careless mistakes.
 a. to making sure
 b. to make sure
 c. to made sure of
 d. make sure of

答：b　ケアレスミスをしないようにできるだけ多く繰り返して答を見直しなさい。

41．to不定詞(1)

「～するために」というto不定詞の副詞的用法に関する問題。aとcでは「to＋動詞の原形」というto不定詞のルールが守られていない。またdではtoが足りないし、c同様、節が後続するのにofがついている。このofは後続するものが名詞（あるいは動名詞）句のときのみ必要となるものであって、that節が来るときはいらない。よって答はb。

42. Freddie Mercury's reputation as a great rock singer rests on his ability ------- emotional depth to his songs.
 a. be giving
 b. is giving
 c. being given
 d. to give

答：d　偉大なロックシンガーとしてのフレディー・マーキュリーの名声は、歌に情熱的な深みを持たせる彼の能力によるものである。

42．to不定詞(2)

to不定詞の形容詞的用法。his ability to give ...「彼の…を与えるという能力」ということになる。このような形容詞的用法は、他の選択肢a、b、cにはない。

43. The State Department urged American citizens ------- to that country, warning that unrest and violence could break out at any time.
 a. not travel
 b. never traveling
 c. not to travel
 d. to not to travel

答：c　国務省は、社会的不安定ひいては暴動がいつでも起こり得ると警告を出し、アメリカ市民にその国へは行かないよう促した。

38

43. to不定詞(3)

　to不定詞を否定の形にする問題。notをtoの前につければよいだけである。きちんとこの形をなしているのはcだけ。ちなみに動名詞を否定するのにも、やはりnotをその直前に置くだけでよい。

---

44. I know students are supposed to study hard, but I don't think we ------- necessarily force them to do so.
    a. had
    b. should
    c. used
    d. have

答：b　学生が一生懸命勉強するべきであるのはわかっているが、必ずしも我々が彼らに無理強いするべきだと私は思わない。

---

44. 助動詞

　助動詞は動詞の原形を取るという基本的なルールに関する問題。副詞necessarilyは構文上、無視して構わない。aとdにあるhad、haveはともに過去分詞（この場合ならforced）と一緒になってそれぞれ現在完了、過去完了を作ることができるが、ここでは原形forceが来ているのでアウト。cのusedも後につながらない。よって答はb。

---

45. Scientists had expected to find about 100,000 genes per person; instead, they found about 30,000—only ------- a fly has, and 10,000 more than a worm.
    a. three times more
    b. the same number of
    c. a little over
    d. twice as many as

答：d　科学者は1人の人間につき約10万の遺伝子が見つかるだろうと予測していたが、約3万しかないことがわかった。これは、ハエの2倍、またミミズより1万多いに過ぎない。

---

45. 〜倍(1)

　「〜倍」というときは、回数（once, twice, three times, etc.）＋as 〜 asであることを覚えておこう。この形がきちんとできているのはdのtwice as many asだけ。よってこれが答。

46. When we talk to someone on the telephone, we tend to concentrate ------- on the conversation.
   a. twice as hard
   b. as seriously as
   c. more severely than
   d. the most vigorous of

答：a　電話で人と話すとき、我々は会話に２倍集中する傾向にある。

46．～倍(2)
　　この文が言いたいのは、「電話では普段より２倍会話に集中する」ということだが、「普段より」というところが省略されている。つまり、twice as hard asの後のas以下が省略されるパターンである。よってaが答。このパターンは会話でも文章中でもよく使われる。b、c、dはどれも意味、形の両方でおかしな文を作ってしまう。

47. The number of air travelers in the nation climbed nearly 10 percent between 1995 and 2000 to ------- .
   a. 200th million
   b. 200 millions
   c. the 200 millionth
   d. 200 million

答：d　国内における飛行機の旅客者の数は1995年と2000年の間に10パーセント増えて２億人になった。

47．数字(1)
　　hundred, thousand, millionなどの語はいずれも数の単位だが、ただ単に数を表すときは決してそれ自体複数形にはならない。e.g. two hundred（100×2でもtwo hundredsにはならない）。「何百もの…」、「何千もの…」というときに、hundreds of ...、thousands of ...となる。問題文では「何百万もの…」というのではなく、ただ単に２億という数字を表しているのだからdが答。

48. Flight 852 for San Francisco is now boarding at ------- .
   a. the Gate Five
   b. Fifth Gate
   c. Gate Five
   d. the Gate Fifth

答：c　サンフランシスコ行き852便は、現在第５ゲートで搭乗中です。

48. 数字(2)

「第〜」という言い方を見る問題。基数を使う場合、ここでの正答cにあるように名詞が先に来てその後に数字が来る。このときtheは不要であることに注意。これに対して序数を使う場合はthe Fifth Gateという順番になり、theが不可欠になる。

---

49. I have an appointment to see the professor on ------- of the month.
    a. the first
    b. one
    c. one date
    d. first date

答：a　私はその月の1日に教授に会う約束がある。

---

49. 数字(3)

日付の問題。いろいろなパターンがあるが、the＋序数を用いて日を言うのが最も正式とされている。e.g. the fourth of July （7月4日）。

---

50. Dorothy Stratten was a young, beautiful, and ------- model when she was killed at the age of 20.
    a. talented
    b. had a lot of talent and a skillful
    c. everybody liked her as a
    d. whose talent was of a

答：a　20の若さで殺されたとき、ドロシー・ストラットンは若くて美しい、才能のあるモデルだった。

---

50. 並列構造(1)

「若くて美しい、才能のあるモデル」というところに注目。young、beautifulに続けるにはやはり形容詞1語にしたほうが、パラレルな構造が保てる。よって答はa。アカデミックな文章では、こういう並列構造が奨励されていて、TOEFLにも頻出の問題である。

Directions: In questions 51-60 each sentence has four underlined words or phrases. The four underlined parts of the sentence are marked a, b, c, and d. Identify the **one** underlined word or phrase that must be changed in order for the sentence to be correct.

51. The professor of <u>molecular biology</u> <u>demanded from</u> his graduate
                              a   b
    students an <u>orderly</u> experiment, a publishable paper, and
                    c
    <u>to work hard.</u>
       d

52. Edward <u>is</u> a <u>physics teacher</u>, a <u>rock guitarist</u>, and a <u>private detection</u>.
             a   b   c   d

53. Mr. Mercury entered the classroom, <u>stood up</u> in front of the students,
                                            a
    and <u>was announcing</u> that he <u>was postponing</u> the exam scheduled
           b   c
    <u>for that day.</u>
        d

54. The final examination <u>will be</u> <u>scoring</u> and <u>evaluated by</u>
                             a   b   c
    <u>all the faculty members.</u>
          d

55. <u>Finishing the paper</u> tonight, <u>it is planned by John</u> <u>to mail it</u>
            a   b   c
    <u>to the journal</u> tomorrow.
       d

56. <u>Accustoming</u> <u>to getting</u> up early, the new teacher <u>found it easy</u> to
        a   b   c
    <u>teach 8 o'clock classes.</u>
         d

57. A <u>true believer in UFOs</u>, <u>it is reported that</u> Mr. Adams has moved to
            a   b
    England <u>in the hope of</u> meeting aliens, <u>who he believes</u> are
               c   d
    responsible for all those crop circles.

58. From 1967 to 1971, Jim Morrison was at the height of his singing
          ──────────   ──
               a   b
career, recorded his six most famous albums.
        ─────────   ────────
             c   d

59. There was a foreign student in Florida, upon leaving his dormitory
        ─────────   ───────
             a   b
for class, immediately got bitten by a mosquito.
─────────   ─────────
    c   d

60. America has avoided two recessions in recent years because of the
                                           ──────────── ──────────────
                                                 a   b
economic growth providing by new technologies.
                ─────────   ────────────
                    c   d

解答 51: d 52: d 53: b 54: b 55: b 56: a 57: b 58: c 59: a 60: c

51. The professor of <u>molecular biology</u> <u>demanded from</u> his graduate students an
　　　　　　　　　　　　　　a　　　　　　　　　b
<u>orderly</u> experiment, a publishable paper, and <u>to work hard</u>.
　c　　　　　　　　　　　　　　　　　　　　　　　　d

答：d（to work hard → hard work）分子生物学の教授は、きちんとした実験、学会誌に掲載されるくらいの論文、そして勤勉さを大学院生たちに要求した。

51. 並列構造(2)

　これも並列構造を問う問題。A, B, and Cという形が見て取れるが、A（an orderly experiment）、B（a publishable paper）ともに純粋な名詞句なのにCだけto不定詞（to work hard）になっている。よってこれも名詞句のhard workにすればよい。

52. Edward <u>is</u> a <u>physics teacher</u>, a <u>rock guitarist</u>, and <u>a private detection</u>.
　　　　　　a　　　　　b　　　　　　　　　c　　　　　　　　　d

答：d（a private detection → a private detective）エドワードは物理教師、ロックギタリスト、そして私立探偵である。

52. 並列構造(3)

　これも3つの名詞句が並ぶパターン。下線部b、c、dともに名詞句であるが、dだけdetection「探知」となっており、detective「探偵」と直される必要がある。そうすれば、b「物理教師」およびc「ロックギタリスト」と意味の上でも並列な構造が確立する。

53. Mr. Mercury entered the classroom, <u>stood up in front of</u> the students, and
　　　　　　　　　　　　　　　　　　　　　　　　a
<u>was announcing</u> that he <u>was postponing</u> the exam <u>scheduled for that day</u>.
　　　b　　　　　　　　　　　　c　　　　　　　　　　　　　　　　d

答：b（was announcing → announced）マーキュリー先生は教室に入り、生徒たちの前に立ち、その日に予定されていた試験を延期すると発表した。

53. 並列構造(4)

　主語Mr. Mercuryに対応する動詞に注目。entered、stood upと来ているのだから、（過去）進行形のwas announcingではなくannouncedにすると、過去形で統一された並列構造が確立する。

54. The final examination <u>will be</u> <u>scoring</u> and <u>evaluated by</u>
　　　　　　　　　　　　　　　　a　　　　b　　　　　　c
<u>all the faculty members</u>.
　　　　　d

答：b（scoring → scored）期末試験はすべての教員によって採点され、評価される。

54. 並列構造(5)

過去分詞がandでつながれるパターン。will be scored and evaluated by …で並列構造を持つ受動態の文にすることができる。

---

55. Finishing the paper tonight, it is planned by John to mail it to the journal tomorrow.
    　　　　　　　　　　a　　　　　　b　　　　　　　　　　c　　　　　　d

答：b（it is planned by John → John plans）ジョンは、今晩その論文を終えて、明日学会誌に送る予定だ。

---

55. 分詞構文(1)

現在分詞が使われる分詞構文であるが、この構文の基本ルールは、分詞（もともとは動詞）の主語と主節の主語が同じであること。ふつう分詞の前に主語は置かれないが、これは主節の主語と同じであるから省略されているのである。このことを頭に入れて問題文を見てみよう。意味の上から論文を終わらせるのはジョンであるはずだが、主節を見ると、仮主語itが主語になっている。このままだとfinishing the paper tonightの主語もitということになり、意味をなさない文になってしまう。bをJohn plansとすれば問題は解決する。（「分詞の意味上の主語は主節の主語と一致する」という分詞構文のルールは、以下の問題56〜59のすべてに当てはまる。）

---

56. Accustoming to getting up early, the new teacher found it easy to teach
    　　　a　　　　　b　　　　　　　　　　　　　　　　　　　c
    8 o'clock classes.
    　　　d

答：a（Accustoming → Accustomed）早起きに慣れているので、その新任教師は8時のクラスを教えるのを苦にしなかった。

---

56. 分詞構文(2)

be accustomed to …「…に慣れている」という、もともと「be＋過去分詞」の表現に関する問題。よって、aがおかしいことがわかる。上で見た現在分詞を使った分詞構文に対して、過去分詞を使った分詞構文と考えるとよい。（主語が統一されていることに注目。「早起きに慣れている」のもthe new teacherであるから、文頭にわざわざこの主語を置くことはないのである。）あるいは本来beingがaccustomedの前にあるのだが、これが省略されてこの形になっているとしてもよい。（しかし、厳密にはbeingをつけた場合と省略した場合とで意味が微妙に変わるようである。興味がある人はネイティブ・スピーカーに確認してみるとよい。）

57. A true believer in UFOs, it is reported that Mr. Adams has moved to England
　　　　　　　　a　　　　　　　　　b
in the hope of meeting aliens, who he believes are responsible for all those
　　　c　　　　　　　　　　　　d
crop circles.

答：b (it is reported that → φ) UFOの真の信者であるアダムズ氏はエイリアンに会いたくてイングランドに引っ越した。というのも、氏はエイリアンがミステリー・サークルを作っていると信じているからだ。

57. 分詞構文(3)

　分詞がないのに分詞構文というのもおかしいが、問題56と同様、being の省略という解釈が成り立つので、一応分詞構文ということにしておく。いずれにせよ、2つの主語が同じであるという分詞構文のルールはここでも保たれる。すなわち、a true believer in UFOs はアダムズ氏であり (i.e. Mr. Adams is a true believer in UFOs)、イングランドに移ったのもアダムズ氏である (i.e. Mr. Adams has moved to England)。よって余分である下線部bを取り去れば、主節でも Mr. Adams が主語になるので、正しい分詞構文ができあがる。

---

58. From 1967 to 1971, Jim Morrison was at the height of his singing career,
　　　　　a　　　　　　　　　　　　　　b
recorded his six most famous albums.
　c　　　　d

答：c (recorded → recording) 1967年から1971年の間、ジム・モリソンは歌手として全盛期にあり、彼の最も有名な6つのアルバムをレコーディングしている。

58. 分詞構文(4)

　文末に現在分詞を持ってきて文をつないでいくパターン。文頭に分詞が来る分詞構文と同様、やはり主語が同じであることに注目。主節の主語は Jim Morrison であり、recording の主語もそうである。また、下線部cの recorded は and he recorded としても文法上おかしくない。問題文にあるようにカンマだけで文がつながれることはないので、cを答として選ぶのは容易であろう。

---

59. There was a foreign student in Florida, upon leaving his dormitory for class,
　　　　a　　　　　　　　　　　　　　　　　　　　b　　　　　　　　　　　　c
immediately got bitten by a mosquito.
　　　　　　d

答：a (There was a → A) あるフロリダの留学生は、授業に行くために寮を出たとたんに蚊に喰われた。

59. 分詞構文(5)

　前置詞uponの後にあるのでleavingは動名詞としたほうがよいのかもしれないが、主節の主語とこのleavingの意味上の主語が同じであることが、「2つの主語を同じに」という分詞構文のルールに重なるので、これにも一応分詞構文の見出しをつけておく。さて、意味を考えると、寮を出るのはフロリダにいる留学生である。また、蚊にさされたのも同じ人物であろうから、主節の主語はa foreign student in Floridaであるべき。よってThere wasを消去し、不定冠詞aを大文字にすれば正しい文が導かれる。

---

60. America has avoided two recessions in recent years because of the economic
　　　　　　　　　　　　　　　　　　　　　　　 ─────────── ─────────
　　　　　　　　　　　　　　　　　　　　　　　　　　　a　　　　　　　b

　　growth providing by new technologies.
　　　　　 ─────────   ───────────────
　　　　　　　　c　　　　　　　　d

答：c（providing → provided）新しいテクノロジーによってもたらされた経済成長のおかげで、アメリカは近年、不況を2度避けることができた。

60. 分詞の形容詞的用法(1)

　現在分詞、過去分詞とも形容詞のように使われることがある。前者は能動的な意味、後者は受身の意味を持つ。また、通例、単独で用いられるときは、普通の形容詞同様、修飾される名詞の前に置かれるが、他のフレーズを伴う場合は、関係節のように、名詞の後に置かれる。さて、問題文であるが、「新しいテクノロジーによってもたらされた経済成長」というのだから、受身のprovidedが正しい分詞の形であろう。また、受身文に特有のby ~というフレーズを伴っているのでeconomic growthを後から修飾するである。

Directions: Questions 61-70 are incomplete sentences. Beneath each sentence, you will see four words or phrases, marked a, b, c, and d. Choose the **one** word or phrase that best completes the sentence.

61. Tom did a presentation for his physics class, hoping to see Mrs. Johnson's ------- smile, but unfortunately, she was sleeping throughout the presentation.

    a. approve
    b. having approved
    c. approving
    d. approved

62. The ------- cars were all severely vandalized by juvenile delinquents in the neighborhood.

    a. parking
    b. parked
    c. park
    d. being parked

63. The new airport opened almost three years ago in the hope that passengers could be ------- away from the increasingly congested international airport nearby.

    a. lures
    b. luring
    c. lured
    d. being lured

64. During the last 10 years, only six new runways ------- at large hub airports in the nation.

    a. have added
    b. might have added
    c. should have been adding
    d. have been added

65. The student suspects were identified ------- some classmates as anti-social troublemakers.

    a. along
    b. together
    c. by
    d. to be

66. ------- saying such a thing before students probably shouldn't have become a teacher in the first place.

   a. Any capable teacher of
   b. Any teacher capable of
   c. Capably any teacher of
   d. Any of teachers capable

67. The detective was initially intrigued by medical reports he found in the files of ------- a minor divorce lawsuit.

   a. what was supposed to be
   b. that was going to be
   c. which
   d. to be believed as

68. The priest first met the college students in their childhood, and ------- then, he has given them moral support.

   a. from
   b. for
   c. since
   d. yet

69. The president has been on the line ------- ; something bad must have happened.

   a. yesterday
   b. in the office last week
   c. since two hours
   d. for more than an hour

70. Norma Arnold says individual attention has worked for ------- fifth-grade daughter and seventh-grade son.

   a. the first time
   b. 20 minutes
   c. herself
   d. her

| 解 答 | 61: c | 62: b | 63: c | 64: d | 65: c | 66: b | 67: a | 68: c | 69: d | 70: d |

61. Tom did a presentation for his physics class, hoping to see Mrs. Johnson's ------- smile, but unfortunately, she was sleeping throughout the presentation.
    a. approve
    b. having approved
    c. approving
    d. approved

答：c　トムはジョンソン先生の満足げな笑顔を期待して物理のクラスでの発表を行ったが、残念なことに、先生は発表の間中居眠りしていた。

61．分詞の形容詞的用法(2)
　　ジョンソン先生の笑顔が問題になっている。この文の意味からいって「認められた」スマイルというより「(よろしいと) 認めてくれる」ような笑顔であるはず。よって能動的な意味を持つ現在分詞の approving が答になる。

62. The ------- cars were all severely vandalized by juvenile delinquents in the neighborhood.
    a. parking
    b. parked
    c. park
    d. being parked

答：b　停まっていた車はすべて近所の不良たちにひどく壊されてしまった。

62．分詞の形容詞的用法(3)
　　日本語では「停まっている車」と言えるが、車の立場になって考えてみれば「(人によって) 停められ」ているのであって、自分の意志で停まっているのではない。よって受身の意味を持つ過去分詞 parked がここでの答になる。

63. The new airport opened almost three years ago in the hope that passengers could be ------- away from the increasingly congested international airport nearby.
    a. lures
    b. luring
    c. lured
    d. being lured

答：c　どんどん混雑がひどくなる近隣の国際空港から利用者を引き寄せようと、その新しい飛行場がオープンされてもう３年になる。

63. 受動態(1)

that節内の主語であるpassengers「乗客たち」の立場になって考えれば、彼らが（何かを）引き寄せるのではなく、彼らが新しい飛行場に引き寄せられる、というのがこの文の意味するところであることがわかる。よって「be＋過去分詞」（受動態）を作るluredが答。

---

64. During the last 10 years, only six new runways ------- at large hub airports in the nation.
    a. have added
    b. might have added
    c. should have been adding
    d. have been added

答：d　ここ10年の間、国内の大きなハブ空港にたったの6つしか新しい滑走路が追加されていない。

---

64. 受動態(2)

これも意味を考えれば簡単に正答が導ける問題。新しい滑走路は自ら何かを追加するのではなく、（人によって）空港に追加されるものである。よって受動態を選べばよい。完了の形になっていて一見ややこしく見えるかも知れないが、be動詞＋過去分詞の形になっているのはdの(have) been addedだけ。

---

65. The student suspects were identified ------- some classmates as anti-social troublemakers.
    a. along
    b. together
    c. by
    d. to be

答：c　生徒である容疑者たちは、クラスメートに反社会的問題児であるとみなされていた。

---

65. 受動態(3)

受動態における「〜によって」というフレーズはbyによって表される。よってcが答になる。ここではbe identified as ...「…とみなされる」におけるasのフレーズがbyのフレーズの後にありややこしく見えるかもしれないが、文脈からこのようなこともしばしば起こるので慣れておいたほうがよい。

66. ------- saying such a thing before students probably shouldn't have become a teacher in the first place.
　　a. Any capable teacher of
　　b. Any teacher capable of
　　c. Capably any teacher of
　　d. Any of teachers capable

答：b　生徒たちの前でそんなことが言える教師は、最初から教師になどなるべきではなかったのだろう。

66．後からの修飾句

　capable はふつうの形容詞として a capable teacher「有能な教師」のように、前から名詞を修飾するが、「～ができる」という意味の capable of の形になると of 以下のフレーズとともに名詞を後から修飾する（分詞の形容詞的用法と同じ特徴：問題60参照）。よって Any teacher capable of (saying such a thing) となる b が答。

67. The detective was initially intrigued by medical reports he found in the files of ------- a minor divorce lawsuit.
　　a. what was supposed to be
　　b. that was going to be
　　c. which
　　d. to be believed as

答：a　探偵は小さな離婚訴訟になるであろうと思われていた一件のファイルの中に見つけた医者の報告書に最初興味をそそられていた。

67．前置詞

　前置詞の後は、名詞句（動名詞のものを含む）であるということがわかっていれば解ける問題。ここでは前置詞 of の後が空所になっているが、選択肢のなかで名詞句を構成できるのは、a の what was supposed to be (a minor divorce lawsuit)「（マイナーな離婚訴訟に）なるであろうと思われていたもの」だけである。先行詞を兼ねた関係代名詞と言われる what が名詞句を作るキーになっている。

68. The priest first met the college students in their childhood and ------- then, he has given them moral support.
   a. from
   b. for
   c. since
   d. yet

答：c　牧師がその大学生たちに会ったのは彼らがまだ子供のころであったが、それ以来彼らに精神的援助をしてきた。

68.　現在完了(1)
　　have＋過去分詞で現在完了だが、この形とともに使われることの多い前置詞（接続詞）は「時」に関わる since と for である。前者は「過去のある1点以来現在まで」、後者は「（現在を含む）〜間」という意味である。ここでの問題では then「そのとき」という過去の1点を指す表現があるので since が答となる。つまり、since then「そのとき以来」ということ。

69. The president has been on the line ------- ; something bad must have happened.
   a. yesterday
   b. in the office last week
   c. since two hours
   d. for more than an hour

答：d　社長は1時間以上も電話に出ている。何か悪いことが起こったに違いない。

69.　現在完了(2)
　　has been があるので、これも現在完了の文。現在完了は過去の表現とは一緒に使えないので、選択肢 a（yesterday）と b（last week）は候補から外れる。問題68で見たように since は「過去のある1点」が後続していれば使えるが、ここでは「2時間」という時間の長さを言う表現が来ているのでアウト（for two hours あるいは since two hours ago であれば OK）。よって答は d の for more than an hour「1時間以上の間」になる。

70. Norma Arnold says individual attention has worked for ------- fifth-grade daughter and seventh-grade son.
   a. the first time
   b. 20 minutes
   c. herself
   d. her

答：d　ノーマ・アーノルドによると、1人1人に注意を払うことが、彼女の5年生の娘と7年生の息子にはよかったのだという。

70. 代名詞(1)

　選択肢 a、b を選ぶとそれぞれ for the first time「初めて」、for 20 minutes「20分間」というフレーズができるが、後続する daughter と son に話がつながっていかなくなる。また、daughter と son はともに可算名詞なので、単数なのに冠詞がないのはおかしい。c の herself でも、文がそこで終わってしまい、fifth-grade daughter and seventh-grade son が宙に浮いてしまう。それに対して、d の her であれば、her fifth-grade daughter and seventh-grade son「彼女の5年生の娘と7年生の息子」ということになり、また所有格は冠詞を必要としないので、意味の上でも文法の上でも万事解決する。

品詞と機能(1)

「品詞」と「機能」という2つの概念は区別されないことが多いが、これはあまり好ましいことではない。以下の例を見られたい。

(1) I have a pencil.
(2) I have a pencil case.

(1)内の目的語 pencil は明らかに名詞である。不定冠詞を伴っているし、また、通例目的語になれるのは名詞のみだからである。(2)の pencil はどうだろう？「名詞の case を修飾しているから形容詞」という答をよく聞く。もしそうなら、比較級、最上級があり、very とも共起できるはずだ。しかし *penciler、*pencilest も *very pencil も存在しない（* は非文法性を表す）。また、SVC の C の位置に入れてみると *This is pencil という非文法的な文章しかできない。一方、(3)と(4)から明らかなように、典型的な形容詞 short はこれらの特徴のすべてを持ち合わす。

(3) short-shorter-shortest / very short
(4) This is short.

よって、(2)における pencil の品詞はやはり名詞ということなる。しかし、確かに case を修飾しているので、この場合、「名詞の pencil が形容詞として機能している」と説明する（言語学的には、もう少し複雑なのだが、本書では難しい話は避ける）。そして、同じようなことが以下の tomorrow にも言える。

(5) I will see her tomorrow.
(6) Tomorrow is my birthday.

(5)だけを見ると、tomorrow は副詞でないかと思ってしまう。しかし、more often、most often、very often に見られるように、ふつうの副詞（ここでは often）には、やはり比較級、最上級があり、また very に修飾され得るという特徴が見られるが、tomorrow には見られない（*more tomorrow、*most tomorrow、*very tomorrow）。また、(6)における tomorrow は主語として機能しているが、ふつう、主語になれるのは名詞だけである。それに、tomorrow's test のように所有格も存在する。これも名詞の特徴である。よって、tomorrow の品詞は名詞ということになる。つまり、(5)の tomorrow も名詞で、ただ、そこでは副詞として機能しているということ。（主語、目的語というのも機能名であり、それらとして機能するのはふつう名詞であることにお気づき願いたい。）おわかりいただけただろうか。

Directions: In questions 71-80 each sentence has four underlined words or phrases. The four underlined parts of the sentence are marked a, b, c, and d. Identify the **one** underlined word or phrase that must be changed in order for the sentence to be correct.

71. Brian Setzer's rockabilly songs, most of which <u>are</u> <u>reminiscent of</u>
                                                                                      a   b
    Elvis Presley, established <u>them</u> as a leading American singer
                                        c
    in <u>the 1980's</u>.
           d

72. The researchers are happy to be <u>at</u> the institute, where they <u>have</u> a
                                                             a   b
    opportunity to conduct <u>unprecedented</u> <u>scientific research</u>.
                                 c   d

73. This story depicts two boys <u>who</u> lost their innocence <u>at a time</u>—the
                                               a   b
    mid-1970's—<u>that</u> Japan <u>was losing</u> its own innocence.
                  c   d

74. <u>In</u> a world <u>which</u> heroes are often <u>in short supply</u>, the story of *Rudy* is
     a   b   c
    an inspirational reminder of the <u>power</u> of the human spirit.
                                           d

75. This is <u>a true story</u> about <u>friendship</u> <u>so that</u> runs <u>deeper than blood</u>.
                 a   b   c   d

76. The lawyer visited St. Mark's Church, where <u>to him</u> <u>had</u> represented
                                              a   b
    <u>a haven</u> <u>throughout</u> so much of his childhood.
       c   d

77. These are the rules and regulations <u>for</u> all the members <u>of</u> this health
                                              a   b
    club <u>must</u> <u>abide by</u>.
        c   d

78. She left early, that was smart, since the party got so wild that the
      ⎯⎯   ⎯⎯⎯⎯⎯⎯⎯
       a   b
   neighbors eventually called the police.
            ⎯⎯⎯⎯⎯⎯⎯⎯⎯⎯⎯⎯⎯⎯ ⎯⎯⎯
                   c   d

79. The political leader is still chasing the ideal of a democratic and free
                        ⎯⎯⎯⎯⎯⎯
                           a
   society in that all persons will live together in harmony and
            ⎯⎯⎯⎯⎯⎯   ⎯⎯⎯⎯⎯⎯⎯⎯⎯
               b   c
   with equal opportunities.
   ⎯⎯⎯⎯⎯⎯⎯⎯⎯⎯⎯⎯⎯⎯⎯⎯⎯
              d

80. While the students were sitting in the cafeteria, they
                       ⎯⎯⎯⎯⎯⎯⎯⎯⎯⎯⎯⎯⎯⎯⎯⎯⎯⎯⎯⎯
                                  a
   noticed a girl eating in a corner booth—a girl her face they could
   ⎯⎯⎯⎯⎯⎯⎯⎯⎯⎯⎯⎯ ⎯⎯⎯⎯⎯⎯⎯⎯⎯⎯⎯⎯   ⎯⎯⎯
          b   c   d
   never forget.

解答 71: c　72: b　73: c　74: b　75: c　76: a　77: a　78: a　79: b　80: d

---

71. Brian Setzer's rockabilly songs, most of which <u>are</u> <u>reminiscent of</u> Elvis Presley,
　　　　　　　　　　　　　　　　　　　　　　　　 a　　　　　 b
established <u>them</u> as a leading American <u>singer in the 1980's</u>.
　　　　　　　 c　　　　　　　　　　　　　　　　 d

答：c（them → him）ブライアン・セッツァーのロカビリー曲は、そのほとんどがエルビス・プレスリーを彷彿させるもので、彼に1980年代におけるアメリカを代表する歌手という地位をもたらした。

---

71. 代名詞(2)

　　代名詞が何を指すかの問題。established以下の意味が「～を1980年代のアメリカを代表する歌手として確立した」というのだから、「～」の位置に入るのは人である。この文の主語はBrian Setzer's rockabilly songsであるから、もしcのようにthemを「～」の位置に入れると「ブライアン・セッツァーのロカビリー曲」が「歌手として確立」されてしまい、おかしなことになる。よってこれをhimにかえ、主語中のBrian Setzerを受けるようにすればよい。

---

72. The researchers are happy to be <u>at</u> the institute, where they have <u>a</u> opportunity
　　　　　　　　　　　　　　　　　　 a　　　　　　　　　　　　　　　　　 b
to conduct <u>unprecedented</u> <u>scientific research</u>.
　　　　　　　 c　　　　　　　　　 d

答：b（a → an）研究者たちは、先例のない科学リサーチを行う機会が得られるその研究所にいられて幸せである。

---

72. 発音

　　opportunityは母音で始まる単語なので、不定冠詞はaではなくan。これは注意さえしていれば簡単に解ける問題であるが、少しややこしいのがuniversityのような単語。これは綴りの上では母音のuで始まる単語だが、その発音は「ウニバーシティ」ではなく「ユニバーシティ」なのでan universityではなくa universityが正解になる。（List 2参照）

---

73. This story depicts two boys <u>who</u> lost their innocence <u>at a time</u>—the mid-1970's
　　　　　　　　　　　　　　　　 a　　　　　　　　　　　　 b
—<u>that</u> Japan <u>was losing</u> its own innocence.
　　 c　　　　　　 d

答：c（that → when）この物語は、1970年代半ば、つまり日本が純潔さを失っていった時代に純潔さを失った2人の少年を描いている。

58

73. 関係副詞(1)

　下線部 c は関係代名詞 that であるが、先行詞になるものが a time「時代」という「時」を表すもので、しかも Japan was losing its own innocence「日本が純潔さを失っていった」という文に「～という時代に」という副詞的意味を加えるものであるから、関係副詞の when が必要となる。

---

74. In a world which heroes are often in short supply, the story of *Rudy* is an
　　　　a　　　b　　　　　　　　　　　c
inspirational reminder of the power of the human spirit.
　　　　　　　　　　　　d

答：b（which → where）よくヒーロー不足が指摘される世界において、「ルーディー」の物語は、人間の精神力を思い起こさせ、やる気にさせてくれる。

---

74. 関係副詞(2)

　下線部 b に続く節から、「ある世界ではヒーローがよく不足する」という意味の文を作ってみると、Heroes are often in short supply in a world ができる。ここで、a world を関係代名詞 which で置き換えると、heroes are often in short supply in which となる。次に先行詞 a world を立て、それに which を前に移動させてこの節をつなぐと、a world which heroes are often in short supply in という形が得られる。ここで大事なのは、最後に in が残ってしまうということ。これは which があくまでも関係代名詞で、名詞句のみを受けるからである。しかしながら、問題文ではこの in がない。ということは関係詞がこの in も含んでいるということ。この機能は、関係副詞 where が持つものである。よって b の which を where に直せばよい。（in which という形も可能：問題 79 参照；「全世界」を指す world については問題 144 参照）

---

75. This is a true story about friendship so that runs deeper than blood.
　　　　　　　　　　a　　　　　　 b　　　　 c　　　　　d

答：c（so that → that）これは、血縁より深い友情についての物語である。

---

75. 関係代名詞(1)

　関係代名詞 that に関する問題。もともと friendship runs deeper than blood「友情が血より深いところを走る（直訳）」という文から作られた関係節なので、so that の構文（問題 179 参照）とは関係がない。that が先行詞 friendship を受ける関係代名詞として働いているのだ。

---

76. The lawyer visited St. Mark's Church, where to him had represented a haven
　　　　　　　　　　　　　　　　　　　　　　　 a　　　 b　　　　　　　　　　　c
throughout so much of his childhood.
　　　　d

答：a（where → which）弁護士は、自分にとって子供時代のほとんどを通じての避難所とも言える場所であったセント・マーク教会を訪れた。

59

76. 関係代名詞(2)

　「セント・マーク教会」というと場所であるから、これを節で修飾するには下線部aにあるように関係副詞whereが必要であると思われるかもしれない。しかし、関係節をよく見てみよう。まず、to himは「彼にとって」という、いわば挿入されたフレーズだから無視する。すると動詞句had representedの直前に関係詞がきていることがわかる。つまり、この関係詞は主語なのだ。そして、（ふつう）名詞のみが主語になるので、ここでの関係詞は副詞のwhereでなく名詞のwhichでないとならない。もともとSt. Mark's Church represented a haven ...という文からこの関係節はできていて、この文中ではSt. Mark's Churchは明らかに主語である。

---

77. These are the rules and regulations <u>for</u> all the members <u>of</u> this health club
　　　　　　　　　　　　　　　　　　　　 a　　　　　　　　　　　　　b
　　<u>must</u> <u>abide by</u>.
　　　c　　　d

答：a（for → that/φ）これが、このヘルスクラブの会員すべてが従わなければならないルールと規則である。

77. 関係代名詞(3)

　この問題文には、abide by「従う」の目的語がない。文全体の意味からしてthe rules and regulationsがその目的語であろうから、目的語が関係代名詞になって前に動いたと考えられる。すると先行詞the rules and regulationsの後にあるforがおかしいことになる。答としてはthatとwhichがあるが、ここでの関係代名詞は限定用法なので前者のほうが好まれる（in whichなど前置詞を伴う場合、およびwho/whose/whomはこの限りでない）。また、目的格の関係代名詞なのでforを消去するだけでもよい（Note 4参照）。

---

78. She left early, <u>that</u> was smart, since the party <u>got so wild</u> that the neighbors
　　　　　　　　　　 a　　　　　　　　　　　　　　　　 b
　　<u>eventually called</u> <u>the</u> police.
　　　　　c　　　　　　d

答：a（that → which）彼女は早く帰ったが、それは賢い選択だった。というのも、パーティーは非常に荒れて、隣人がついには警察を呼ぶまでに至ったからだ。

78. 関係代名詞(4)

　書き言葉では、2つの文章をカンマだけでつなぐことは許されない。このことからShe left early, that was smart「彼女が早く帰った、それが賢かった」の部分がおかしいことがわかる。この場合、smart「賢い」のは「彼女が早く帰った」という前文のすべてを指す。このように文全体を受ける関係代名詞はthatではなくwhichである。この特徴はthatにはなく、よって問題文のthatは、「それ」という指示詞としかみなされない。この指示詞をどうしても活かそうというのであれば、and that was smartとでもするしかない。

> 79. The political leader is still chasing the ideal of a democratic and free society in
> _____a_____
> that all persons will live together in harmony and with equal opportunities.
> ___b___   ___c___   _____d_____
> 答：b（that → which）その政治的指導者は、万人が仲よく平等な機会を持って一緒に暮らすという民主的自由社会の理想を今でも追い求めている。

79．関係代名詞(5)

　関係代名詞を使ったため、文が前置詞で終わってしまうことがある。e.g. the house which we live in「私たちが住む家」。このときしばしば前置詞を関係代名詞の前に移すという作業が行われるが（i.e. the house in which we live）、関係代名詞がthatの場合だけは例外で、in thatのような形はありえない。よって、下線bのthatをwhichに直す必要がある（Note 5参照）。

> 80. While the students were sitting in the cafeteria, they noticed a girl eating in a
> _____a_____   ___b___   ___c___
> corner booth—a girl her face they could never forget.
>   ___d___
> 答：d（her → whose）カフェテリアに座っている間、その学生たちはある女の子が角のブースで食事しているのに気がついた。彼らには決して忘れられない顔であった。

80．関係代名詞(6)

　後半にあるa girl her face「少女、彼女の顔」のところがつながらないことは一目瞭然。「彼らが決して忘れられない顔の少女」というようにつなぐには、やはり関係代名詞が必要。ここでは「彼女の（顔）」というのだから所有格のwhoseが答である。

Directions: Questions 81-90 are incomplete sentences. Beneath each sentence, you will see four words or phrases, marked a, b, c, and d. Choose the **one** word or phrase that best completes the sentence.

81. One of my favorite scenes in the movie is ------- Rudy arrives at the University of Notre Dame without even applying to the university.

    a. that
    b. there
    c. where
    d. what

82. The professor let us copy for our movie some of his framed degrees and -------.

    a. memorabilia other of his long career
    b. memorabilia other than long his career
    c. other memorabilia long career of his
    d. other memorabilia of his long career

83. He offered ------- at the death of her mother.

    a. his sympathy heartfelt
    b. his heartfelt sympathy
    c. heartfelt of his sympathy
    d. sympathy of his heartfelt

84. *Rocky*, one of the best motion pictures of the 1970's, ------- the actor Sylvester Stallone.

    a. written by
    b. written was by
    c. was written by
    d. by

85. My father's company does random testing of its products ------- .

    a. for quality control
    b. by reason of control quality
    c. in order for controlling
    d. in such a quality that control

86. For the election scheduled for next month, the majority of voters ------- independents.

   a. had been
   b. have been
   c. must have been
   d. will be

87. Hideki asked the professor whether or not she ------- the word "competence."

   a. will know
   b. has known
   c. knew
   d. may know

88. Not once, in any of these amusement parks, ------- with big crowds.

   a. we had to compete
   b. have had we to compete
   c. had to we compete
   d. did we have to compete

89. Only with a bank loan ------- .

   a. he will be able to buy a house
   b. will he be able to buy a house
   c. will be he able to buy a house
   d. will be able to he buy a house

90. It is obligatory that a foreign student ------- the international student advisor before signing up for any class.

   a. see
   b. sees
   c. to see
   d. seeing

| 解答 | 81: c | 82: d | 83: b | 84: c | 85: a | 86: d | 87: c | 88: d | 89: b | 90: a |

81. One of my favorite scenes in the movie is ------- Rudy arrives at the University of Notre Dame without even applying to the university.
    a. that
    b. there
    c. where
    d. what

答：c　その映画の私の大好きなシーンの1つは、ルーディーが願書も出さずにノートルダム大学に到着するところである。

81．先行詞を兼ねた関係詞

　what、where、when等はそれぞれ「もの、こと」、「ところ」、「とき」を自ら表し、先行詞を兼ねた関係詞として働くことができる。問題67ではwhatの例を見たが、ここで要求されているのは、「ルーディーが願書を出すことさえせずにノートルダム大学に到着するところ」という意味からwhere「ところ」である。

82. The professor let us copy for our movie some of his framed degrees and ------- .
    a. memorabilia other of his long career
    b. memorabilia other than long his career
    c. other memorabilia long career of his
    d. other memorabilia of his long career

答：d　教授は、我々の映画のために、額に入った学位と彼の長い経歴における他の記念の品のコピーを作らせてくれた。

82．逆順のパターン(1)

　TOEFLでは、正しい語順とは逆のものの出題もよく見られるので、慣れておくとよい。まず、aであるがmemorabiliaとotherの位置が逆。bでは、longとhisが逆（his longの順番になっていたとしても全体の意味がおかしいが）。cは、other memorabiliaとlong career of hisがつながらない。よって、答はd。（copyの目的語にあたるsome of his framed degrees and other memorabilia of his long careerは、Heavy NP-Shiftにより文末に来ている：問題5およびNote 1参照。）

83. He offered ------- at the death of her mother.
   a. his sympathy heartfelt
   b. his heartfelt sympathy
   c. heartfelt of his sympathy
   d. sympathy of his heartfelt

答：b 彼は、彼女の母親の死に際して心から同情した。

83. 逆順のパターン(2)

　　heartfelt「心からの、深く感じた」は、(限定的にしか使われない) 形容詞なので、被修飾語の sympathy の前にないとおかしい。よって a はアウト。正しい「形容詞＋名詞」の語順ができている b が答となる。また、A of B「BのA」という形では、AもBも名詞でなくてはならないが、c と d は形容詞 heartfelt が関わっているのでまずい。その上、d の his heartfelt は、「所有格の後は名詞」というルールからいってもおかしい (Note 6 参照)。また、この手の問題としては、句動詞が逆順になっているものもある (e.g. off turn → turn off)。

84. *Rocky*, one of the best motion pictures of the 1970's, ------- the actor Sylvester Stallone.
   a. written by
   b. written was by
   c. was written by
   d. by

答：c　1970年代最高の映画の１つであるロッキーは、俳優シルベスター・スタローンによって書かれた物語である。

84. 逆順のパターン(3)

　　be動詞＋過去分詞＋by という受動態の形がきちんとできているのは c だけ。b は was と written の語順が逆である。a には be動詞がないし、d に至ってはまったく動詞がない。よって答は c。

85. My father's company does random testing of its products ------- .
   a. for quality control
   b. by reason of control quality
   c. in order for controlling
   d. in such a quality that control

答：a　父の会社は、品質管理のために製品をランダムにテストしている。

85. 逆順のパターン(4)

quality control「品質管理」という複合語が決め手となる。bはこの語順が逆になっているのでアウト。cでは、in orderの後にto不定詞ではなくforが来ているし、動名詞のcontrolling（他動詞）にも、目的語が欠けている。dは、接続詞thatの後に節が来ていない。答はa。

---

86. For the election scheduled for next month, the majority of voters ------- independents.
    a. had been
    b. have been
    c. must have been
    d. will be

答：d　来月予定されている選挙では、投票者の大部分を無党派層が占めるだろう。

86. 時制(1)

「来月予定されている選挙」というのだから、未来の話。よってwillを使ったdが答になる。選択肢aは過去完了、bは現在完了。cのmust have＋過去分詞は「〜したに違いない」という意味なのでいずれもアウト。

---

87. Hideki asked the professor whether or not she ------- the word "competence."
    a. will know
    b. has known
    c. knew
    d. may know

答：c　秀樹は教授に"competence"という単語を知っているか尋ねた。

87. 時制(2)

時制の一致の問題。主節の動詞が過去形の場合にのみ、自動的に従属節の動詞も過去になるが、これを時制の一致という。ここでの主節の動詞は過去形のasked。よって答はcのknew。主節の動詞が現在形である場合はこの限りでなく、従属節の動詞の時制は現在形でも過去形でもあり得る。

---

88. Not once, in any of these amusement parks, ------- with big crowds.
    a. we had to compete
    b. have had we to compete
    c. had to we compete
    d. did we have to compete

答：d　これらのどの遊園地でも、1度たりとも混雑にもまれる必要はなかった。

88. 強調の倒置(1)

この文に見られるように、否定の表現（ここでは not once）が強調のため文頭に置かれると、主語と助動詞の間に倒置が起こる。もともと文中に助動詞がない場合は、時制に応じたさまざまな do の形を使うことになる。答は d。(have to「〜しなければならない」の have は現在完了のそれと違い、一般動詞。よって倒置には関与しない。) もうひとつ例を挙げておこう。He never came back to Japan again. → Never again did he come back to Japan.「彼は 2 度と日本には戻らなかった。」この倒置構文によく使われる他の否定表現として、hardly、rarely、seldom そして no sooner ... than があるので、まとめて覚えておくとよい。

---

89. Only with a bank loan ------- .
    a. he will be able to buy a house
    b. will he be able to buy a house
    c. will be he able to buy a house
    d. will be able to he buy a house

答：b　銀行からのローンによってのみ、彼は家を買えるだろう。

---

89. 強調の倒置(2)

問題 88 で見た強調の倒置は、確かに否定表現に多いのだが、問題 89 からわかるように、only のような表現にも適用されることがある。ここでもメカニズムは同じ。まず、強調のために only with a bank loan が文頭に移動する。次に主語と助動詞の間に倒置が起こる。今回はもともと will があるので、これが倒置に関与するだけ。よって答は b (Note 2 参照)。

---

90. It is obligatory that a foreign student ------- the international student advisor before signing up for any class.
    a. see
    b. sees
    c. to see
    d. seeing

答：a　外国人学生は、どのクラスの科目登録をするにも、まずインターナショナル・スチューデント・アドバイザーに会わなくてはならない。

---

90. 命令・要求のときの原形(1)

It is obligatory that ...「…は義務である」というのは、言い換えれば「…せよ」という命令・要求の表現である。このとき、that 節内の動詞は原形にするというのがルール。obligatory の他にも、この It is ~ that の形を取って命令・要求の意味を表す形容詞も多いので、リストで確認しておこう (List 3 参照)。

Directions: In questions 91-100 each sentence has four underlined words or phrases. The four underlined parts of the sentence are marked a, b, c, and d. Identify the **one** underlined word or phrase that must be changed in order for the sentence to be correct.

91. The professor suggested that the lazy student <u>stopped</u> <u>coming</u> to her
                     a   b
    class <u>because</u> he wasn't <u>studying at all.</u>
       c   d

92. <u>Noting</u> a racial remark in a speech by a famous comedian, John said
     a
    <u>to himself,</u> "That is one of <u>more</u> foolish statements I have <u>ever</u>
     b   c   d
    heard."

93. <u>The actress</u> is beautiful, and she <u>uses</u> her beauty <u>to</u> the <u>most fullest.</u>
     a   b   c   d

94. <u>Good</u> coaches <u>much knowledge</u> of their <u>sports</u> <u>thoroughly.</u>
     a   b   c   d

95. <u>With two atoms</u> <u>of</u> hydrogen combine with <u>one of oxygen</u> to form
       a   b   c
    <u>water.</u>
     d

96. Jimi Hendrix attempted <u>to prove</u> that rock music <u>as</u> <u>a</u> form of <u>art.</u>
            a   b c   d

97. Many business people <u>in</u> Japan are <u>now learning</u> <u>communicative</u>
            a   b   c
    English in order to remain <u>competition.</u>
              d

98. <u>The photographer</u> often makes his <u>family members</u> <u>as</u> his <u>subjects.</u>
       a   b   c   d

99. Hard work will continue to make it possible the realization of his
    ───────   ─────── ──   ──────────────
       a   b   c   d
    numerous dreams.

100. My solutions to the problems were the same to the teacher's.
     ──   ──   ──   ──────────
      a   b   c   d

| 解　答 | 91: a | 92: c | 93: d | 94: b | 95: a | 96: b | 97: d | 98: c | 99: c | 100: c |

91. The professor suggested that the lazy student <u>stopped</u> <u>coming</u> to her class
 　　　　　　　　　　　　　　　　　　　　　　　　　　a　　　　b
<u>because</u> he wasn't <u>studying at all.</u>
　c　　　　　　　　　d

答：a（stopped → stop）教授は、その怠惰な学生がまったく勉強していないので、授業に来るなと言った。

91. 命令・要求のときの原形(2)

　動詞suggestも that節を伴ったときには、この問題文のように「命令・要求」の意味を持つことがある。この場合that節内の動詞は原形。suggestの他にも同じ特徴を持つ動詞があるので覚えておこう（List 4参照）。

92. Noting <u>a</u> racial remark in a speech by a famous comedian, John said <u>to himself,</u>
　　　　a　　　　　　　　　　　　　　　　　　　　　　　　　　　　　　　b
"That is one of <u>more</u> foolish statements I have <u>ever heard.</u>"
　　　　　　　　c　　　　　　　　　　　　　　　d

答：c（more → the most）有名なコメディアンによるスピーチの中に人種差別的な発言を聞いたとき、ジョンは「あれは今まで聞いた中で最も馬鹿らしいステートメントの1つだ」と独り言を言った。

92. 最上級(1)

　one of ＋最上級で「最も～な1つ」というパターン。また、theを伴うのも、ふつう比較級ではなく、最上級に見られる特徴（例外の1つとして問題200参照）。よって下線部cのmoreをmostにする。

93. <u>The</u> actress is beautiful, and she <u>uses</u> her beauty <u>to</u> the <u>most fullest.</u>
　　　a　　　　　　　　　　　　　　　b　　　　　　　　c　　　　　d

答：d（most fullest → fullest）その女優は美しく、そして自分の美を十分に利用している。

93. 最上級(2)

　mostは-estを伴えない形容詞および副詞について最上級を作る。よって、もともと-estを伴えるfullにはつく必要がない。most fullestは、単にfullestにするべき。（同じことが、比較級のmoreと-erについても言える。）

94. Good coaches much knowledge of their sports thoroughly.
　　　　a　　　　　　b　　　　　　　　c　　　　d
答：b（much knowledge of → know）よいコーチは、自分のスポーツを完全に把握している。

94．S＋V(1)
　主語の後には動詞が来る。この基本的なことが、TOEFLでは必ずチェックされる。さて、問題94には動詞がない。Good coachesが複数の主語であるから、それに合わせて名詞knowledgeと派生関係にある動詞knowを導き出し、下線部bと置き換えればよい。

95. With two atoms of hydrogen combine with one of oxygen to form water.
　　　　a　　　　b　　　　　　　　　　　　　c　　　　　　　d
答：a（With two atoms → Two atoms）水素原子2つが酸素原子1つと結びついて水を作る。

95．S＋V(2)
　問題95には主語がない。動詞combineの前にあるのは「水素原子2つと一緒に」という前置詞句。ふつう主語は名詞句なので、これでは正しいS＋Vの形ができない。解決策は簡単。この場合、前置詞withを削除するだけで、「水素原子2つが」という主語ができあがる。

96. Jimi Hendrix attempted to prove that rock music as a form of art.
　　　　　　　　　　　　　　　a　　　　　　　　　b c　　　　d
答：b（as → was）ジミ・ヘンドリクスは、ロック音楽が芸術の1形態であることを証明しようとした。

96．S＋V(3)
　節である以上、従属節の中にも主語と動詞があってしかるべき。しかしながら、問題96の従属節には動詞が見当たらない。「ロック音楽が芸術の1形態である」という意味からして、be動詞が必要である。時制の一致（問題87参照）を踏まえてwasとすることができれば合格。

97. Many business people in Japan are now learning communicative English in
　　　　　　　　　　　　　　a　　　　　　　　b　　　　　　　c
　order to remain competition.
　　　　　　　　　d
答：d（competition → competitive）今、日本の多くのビジネス人が、競争力を保とうとしてコミュニカティブ・イングリッシュを習っている。

97. SVC

　remain は be 動詞や become、appear、seem、stay などの一般動詞と同様に、SVC の構文を作る。この場合、John（S）became（V）rich（C）「ジョンがリッチになった」の例からもわかるように、S＝C、すなわち「ジョン＝リッチ」という関係が成り立つ。さて、問題文であるが、remain の意味上の主語は「日本の多くのビジネス人」であり、C の位置に来る単語が competition「競争」であると、「人＝競争」というおかしなことになってしまう。よってこれを competitive「競争力のある、他に負けない」という形容詞にして、many business people in Japan = competitive という正しい関係にしてやる必要がある。

98. The photographer often makes his family members as his subjects.
　　　　　a　　　　　　　　　　　　　　b　　　　c　　　d

答：c（as → φ）その写真家は、しばしば自分の家族を被写体にする。

98. SVOC (1)

　SVOC の文型では、O＝C の関係が成り立つ。問題文では、his family members = his subjects となればよいのだから、as がいらないだけである。

99. Hard work will continue to make it possible the realization of his numerous
　　　　a　　　　　　　　　　　b　　c　　　　　　　　d
　 dreams.

答：c（it → φ）勤勉が、彼の数え切れない夢をかなえ続けるだろう。

99. SVOC (2)

　少しややこしい文構造である。SVOC の文の中には、to 不定詞を受ける it が O の位置に来て、makes it possible to ...「…するのを可能にする」というパターンも見られるが、問題 99 では、to 不定詞がないので、この可能性はない。意味の上から考えると、possible「可能」なのは the realization of his numerous dreams「彼の数え切れない夢の実現」で、そうだとすれば、OC という語順から、the realization of his numerous dreams（O）possible（C）となるのがふつうである。実際、これが本来あるべき形なのだが、このままだと、比較的長い O に対して、1 語のみの C という「頭でっかち」な構造ができてしまう。英語はもともと頭でっかちを嫌う言語（仮主語の it などはこの特徴を示すいい例）なので、ここでも O と C の間に逆転が起こり、文の座りをよくしているのである（つまり、Heavy NP-Shift：問題 5 参照）。

100. My solutions to the problems were the same to the teacher's.
　　　ａ　　　　　　ｂ　　　　　　　　　　　ｃ　　ｄ

答：c（to → as）その問題の私の解決法は、先生のと同じだった。

100．same as
　sameといつもペアになって出て来るのがasであり、sameasをまとめて覚えておけば問題ない。

Directions: Questions 101-110 are incomplete sentences. Beneath each sentence, you will see four words or phrases, marked a, b, c, and d. Choose the **one** word or phrase that best completes the sentence.

101. These chemistry textbooks are the same size ------- those physics ones.

   a. of
   b. to
   c. that of
   d. as

102. Mudslides and collapsed buildings have effectively blocked the roads, keeping needed aid ------- the thousands of people left homeless by the big earthquake.

   a. from reaching
   b. to arrive
   c. in get to
   d. entered

103. John is now at a point in his life where he is looking forward ------- .

   a. to get married
   b. to retiring and playing golf
   c. with his wife and children
   d. with regard

104. ------- many tourist attractions, this one is like nature's amusement park and will surely blow your mind.

   a. A like
   b. It is unlikely
   c. It is not like
   d. Unlike

105. ------- we think the Asian economic crisis ended in 1999, there remain signs that indicate otherwise.

   a. Even
   b. It is
   c. Even though
   d. There is

106. Those young gangsters, who at that time had been from 16 to 18 -------, never made it past the age of 30.

    a. years of old
    b. old years
    c. years of age
    d. ages

107. We have ------- seen such an effective teacher as she has proven herself to be.

    a. sure
    b. rarely
    c. everly
    d. certain

108. The Linguistics Department ------- experts in formal semantics and computational linguistics.

    a. needs to seriously
    b. needs to be hired serious
    c. is in serious need of
    d. seriously need more

109. ------- universities in that country are already offering computational linguistics programs on the web.

    a. The number of
    b. A number of
    c. A large amount of
    d. The large amount of

110. Thomas Edison was ------- his love of books when he was little.

    a. very famous as
    b. famous enough to
    c. known well into
    d. well known for

| 解　答 | 101: d　102: a　103: b　104: d　105: c　106: c　107: b　108: c　109: b　110: d |

101. These chemistry textbooks are the same size ------- those physics ones.
    a. of
    b. to
    c. that of
    d. as

答：d　これらの化学の教科書は、あれらの物理の教科書と同じサイズである。

101．same〜as

　基本的に問題100と同じで、sameと来たら自然にasが思い浮かぶようにしておけば答えられる問題。今回は、sameとasが連続するのではなく間にsizeという単語が入っているが、sameとasがセットをなすことには変わりない。英作文にも使えるパターンだから覚えておこう。

102. Mudslides and collapsed buildings have effectively blocked the roads, keeping needed aid ------- the thousands of people left homeless by the big earthquake.
    a. from reaching
    b. to arrive
    c. in get to
    d. entered

答：a　泥流と崩壊した建物が事実上道をふさいでしまい、大地震でホームレスになった何千もの人々に必要な援助が届くのを妨げていた。

102．keep A from B

　keep A from B という決まった形。fromは前置詞だから、Bに来るものは名詞あるいは動名詞で、「AからB（名詞）を隠す」、あるいは「AがB（動名詞）するのを妨げる」といった意味を持つ。ここでは、選択肢aのみがこの形を導く。また、keepはSVOCの形も取ることが可能で、dのenteredは過去分詞であるから、見かけ上needed aidがO、enteredがCという分析ができる。しかし、この分析には意味の上で無理があるし、the thousands of 以降にもつながって行かず、やはりアウトである。

103. John is now at a point in his life where he is looking forward ------- .
    a. to get married
    b. to retiring and playing golf
    c. with his wife and children
    d. with regard

答：b　ジョンは、今や引退してゴルフをすることを実際に楽しみにできる年齢である。

103．look forward to

これも成句の1つ。look forward to における to は、前置詞であって to 不定詞の to ではない。よって後に来るのは名詞あるいは動名詞句。これらの条件を満たすのは選択肢 b のみ。同じように object to「〜に反対する」、confess to「〜したことを白状する」における to も前置詞なので、まとめて覚えておこう。

104. ------- many tourist attractions, this one is like nature's amusement park and will surely blow your mind.
    a. Alike
    b. It is unlikely
    c. It is not like
    d. Unlike

答：d　多くの観光名所とは違い、これは自然の遊園地であり、きっとあなたはびっくりするだろう。

104．(un) like vs. alike

like およびその反意語の unlike は前置詞で、後に必ず名詞句が来る。これに対し alike は常に叙述的に使われる形容詞であるから、A and B are alike.「A と B は似ている」とは言えても、限定的に A is alike B とは言えない（Note 6 参照）。よって alike が前から many tourist attractions を修飾することなどないので a は候補から外れる。It is unlikely は、主に（that）節を取るので b もアウト。c を選ぶと、まず it が指すものがわからなくなる。その上、2つの節がカンマのみでつながれることになるので、これもまずい。よって、答は前置詞の unlike。

105. ------- we think the Asian economic crisis ended in 1999, there remain signs that indicate otherwise.
    a. Even
    b. It is
    c. Even though
    d. There is

答：c　アジアの経済危機は1999年に終わったと我々は思っているが、そうではないと示唆する印がまだ見られる。

105．接続詞

この文には節が2つあり、これをつなぐには接続詞が必要である。a の even は「〜さえ」という強調語。また、b と d はともに S＋V であり、接続詞ではない。よって答は c の even though。though は逆接の接続詞で、even を伴って「たとえ〜（する）にしても」という意味になる。

106. Those young gangsters, who at that time had been from 16 to 18 ------- , never made it past the age of 30.
   a. years of old
   b. old years
   c. years of age
   d. ages

答：c　当時年齢が16から18であったあの若いギャングメンバーたちは、30まで生きることはなかった。

106．years of age
　客観的に年齢を表す言い方。より一般的なyears oldに加えて覚えておこう。また、「〜歳のときに」という場合は、単にatかat the age ofを使う。

107. We have ------- seen such an effective teacher as she has proven herself to be.
   a. sure
   b. rarely
   c. everly
   d. certain

答：b　彼女は実践して見せてくれたが、我々は彼女ほど効果的な教育をする教師をめったに見たことがない。

107．副詞 vs. 形容詞
　形容詞は名詞を修飾するが、副詞は用言（動詞、形容詞等）を修飾する。この問題文ではsee(n)「見る」という動詞を修飾するのだから、副詞が必要。aのsureとdのcertainは形容詞だからアウト。cにあるeverlyなどという語は存在しない。よって答はbの副詞rarely。

108. The Linguistics Department ------- experts in formal semantics and computational linguistics.
   a. needs to seriously
   b. needs to be hired serious
   c. is in serious need of
   d. seriously need more

答：c　言語学科は、形式意味論とコンピュータ言語学の専門家を非常に必要としている。

108. in need of

　in need of は、need を名詞として使った「〜が必要である」という表現。もちろん need が動詞として使われることも多い。その場合は、他動詞であるから直後に目的語が来る。選択肢 a では、to seriously が邪魔。b では、「言語学科が雇われる必要がある」というあり得ない意味と、serious 以下が文の前半につながらない。d でも need が動詞として使われているが、単数主語なのに三単現の -s がないのでアウト。よって答は c（Note 7 参照）。

109. ------- universities in that country are already offering computational linguistics programs on the web.
　　a. The number of
　　b. A number of
　　c. A large amount of
　　d. The large amount of

答：b　その国の多くの大学が、すでにウェブ上でコンピュータ言語学のプログラムを提供している。

109. a number of, etc.

　a number of は、可算名詞について「多くの」という意味をなす。c と d にある amount を使うと、意味は同じでも不可算名詞を修飾することになる。ここでは可算名詞 universities が被修飾語なので、c と d はアウト。また、the number of になると「〜の数」という意味の単数主語を作ることになるので注意。問題文中の動詞は are であるから、主語は「多くの大学」という複数でなければならない。よって、答は b。

110. Thomas Edison was ------- his love of books when he was little.
　　a. very famous as
　　b. famous enough to
　　c. known well into
　　d. well known for

答：d　トーマス・エジソンは、子供のとき、無類の本好きであったことで有名だ。

110. known for

　選択肢 a を選ぶと、「エジソンは彼の本への愛情としてとても有名だった」、すなわち、Edison = his love of books というおかしなことになる。b にある famous enough to には何らかの動詞の原形が後続して his love of books をその目的語としないと文がつながらない。c にある known well into は存在しない言い方。よって、答は d。「〜で知られている」というときは前置詞に for を使う。be well known for を「〜で有名だ」という意味の成句として覚えてもよい。（well known は「有名な」という意味の形容詞（well-known）であると分析されることもある。）

Directions: In questions 111-120 each sentence has four underlined words or phrases. The four underlined parts of the sentence are marked a, b, c, and d. Identify the **one** underlined word or phrase that must be changed in order for the sentence to be correct.

111. They <u>handled</u> the chemical with a great deal of <u>cautions</u>, <u>since</u> it was
          a   b   c
     known to be very <u>explosive</u>.
                          d

112. This <u>drug</u> is <u>effective</u>, but it takes a <u>long</u> time to <u>act</u> the pain.
           a   b   c   d

113. That Korean student, <u>along</u> with <u>others</u> from Taiwan, <u>are</u> to <u>visit</u> the
                                  a   b   c   d
     nursery to entertain the children there.

114. The computer company has <u>yet</u> notified <u>most</u> of the 3,000 people who
                                             a   b
     <u>will lose</u> their jobs as <u>part of</u> a cost-cutting campaign.
         c   d

115. Bored <u>with</u> the lecture, the student <u>dreamed up</u> a classroom prank,
        a   b   c
     more for diversion than any <u>another</u> reason.
                                    d

116. The <u>practice</u> of <u>bribing</u> that went on <u>between the two companies</u>
            a   b   c
     appears <u>having peaked</u> about two years ago.
                 d

117. The <u>single most important</u> <u>change</u> for the English Program will be to
              a   b
     hire <u>more</u> quickly as possible only teachers who are capable of
          c
     <u>speaking the language</u>.
             d

118. Here, as on Japan, reactions to the film were far from subdued.
       a   b   c   d

119. How to be more competitive is a question that is normally associated
      a   b   c
    by men.
    d

120. When the professor made two contradictory remarks, students began
             a   b
    to the questions the credibility of her lecture.
            c   d

解 答　111: b　112: d　113: c　114: a　115: d　116: b　117: c　118: b　119: d　120: c

111. They handled the chemical with a great deal of cautions, since it was known to
　　　　　　　a　　　　　　　　　　　　　　b　　　　　c
be very explosive.
　　　　d

答：b（cautions → caution）彼らは、その化学薬品をとても注意深く扱った。というのも、その薬品はとても爆発しやすいことで知られていたからだ。

111. a great deal of

　　この表現はふつう不可算名詞とともにしか使われない。よって、bの複数名詞cautionsをcautionにし、a great deal of caution「たくさんの注意をもって」とする。また、基本的に同じ意味を表すa good deal ofは肯定文にのみ使われるが、a great deal ofはこの限りでない。

112. This drug is effective, but it takes a long time to act the pain.
　　　　a　　　　　　　b　　　　　　　　c　　　　　　　d

答：d（act → act on）この薬は効果的であるが、痛みに効くのに長い時間がかかる。

112. act on

　　この文におけるactは目的語the painが後続しているので他動詞ということになるが、他動詞actの意味は「～を演じる、～のような振る舞いをする」というもの。「～に効く」というときは、act onという形になる。ちなみに、act upは「（子供などが）あばれる、いたずらする」という意味。

113. That Korean student, along with others from Taiwan, are to visit the nursery to
　　　　　　　　　　　　　　　a　　　　　b　　　　　　　c　　d
entertain the children there.

答：c（are → is）あの韓国人学生は、台湾からの他の学生たちとともに、託児所に行って子供たちを喜ばせる予定だ。

113. along with

　　この文の理屈から言えば、託児所を訪れるのは1人の韓国人学生と数人の台湾からの学生たち。つまり、複数である。しかし、along with「～と一緒に、～を伴って」に導かれるフレーズは、文法上主語の数には影響を与えないことを覚えておこう。よって、主語はthat Korean studentのみなので、動詞はareではなくisが正解。同じような意味を持つ以下の表現に導かれるフレーズも主語の一部にはならない。together with、accompanied by、as well as。

114. The computer company has <u>yet</u> notified <u>most of</u> the 3,000 people who <u>will lose</u>
　　　　　　　　　　　　　　　　a　　　　　　　　b　　　　　　　　　　　　　　　　c
　　　their jobs as <u>part of</u> a cost-cutting campaign.
　　　　　　　　　　d

答：a（yet → already）そのコンピュータ会社は、コスト削減キャンペーンの一環として仕事を失う3,000人のほとんどにすでに通達している。

114．already vs. yet

　alreadyは肯定文に、yetは否定文と疑問文に使うという基本に関する問題。この文は肯定文だし、文末に来るべきyetがhasとnotifiedの間にあるのはおかしい。has/be yet to ...「まだ…していない」というパターンもあるが、この場合はto不定詞が必要になる。この問題文にはそれがないので、やはりyetをalreadyに換えるしかない。

115. <u>Bored</u> <u>with</u> the lecture, the student <u>dreamed up</u> a classroom prank, more for
　　　　a　　b　　　　　　　　　　　　　　　　　c
　　　diversion than any <u>another</u> reason.
　　　　　　　　　　　　　　　d

答：d（another → other）講義に飽きて、その学生は教室でのいたずらを思いついたが、気晴らしのためという理由以外の何物でもなかった。

115．any other

　問題文に見られるように、any otherは比較級においてよく見られ、比較の対象物が単数の場合は必ず単数名詞を伴って「他のどの～」という意味になる（ここではdiversionが単数なのでreasonも単数）。any anotherという表現はない。

116. The <u>practice</u> <u>of bribing</u> that went on <u>between the two companies</u> appears
　　　　　a　　　　b　　　　　　　　　　　　　　　　c
　　　<u>having peaked</u> about two years ago.
　　　　　　d

答：d（having peaked → to have peaked）両社における贈収賄の慣習は、約2年前がピークであったようである。

116．appear to

　appearは、動名詞でなくto不定詞を取る動詞の1つ。文法的にも、意味の上でも同じ特徴を持つseem to「～のようだ」、be likely to「～しそうだ」とセットにして覚えておくとよい（List 5参照）。

117. The single most important change for the English Program will be to hire more
         ───────────   ──────   ────
              a   b   c
quickly as possible only teachers who are capable of speaking the language.
                                                     ───────────────────
                                                              d

答：c（more → as）英語学科にとっての最も重要な改革は、できるだけはやく、英語を話せる教師のみを雇うことであろう。

117. as ～ as

　　as quickly as possible で「できるだけはやく」。この文でも hire「雇う」の目的語（only teachers who are capable of speaking the language）が長いので、文末に移っている（i.e. Heavy NP-Shift：Note 1 参照）。

118. Here, as on Japan, reactions to the film were far from subdued.
     ──── ──   ──────────   ─────────────────
      a   b   c   d

答：b（on → in）日本と同様ここでも、その映画に対する反応は静かなものなんかではなかった。

118. as in

　　厳密に言うと「日本（の中）でと同様にここでも（つまり、この国でも）」である。「日本（の中）で」というのは on Japan でなく in Japan であるから、as in Japan ということになる。もちろん他の前置詞を伴う表現であれば、それが使われることになる。e.g. as on some coins「いくつかのコイン（の表面）に見られるように」

119. How to be more competitive is a question that is normally associated by men.
     ─────   ──────────────   ────────   ──
        a   b   c   d

答：d（by → with）いかにより競争力を持てるようになれるかというのは、通常男性のものとされる問題である。

119. associate A with B

　　associate A with B で「A と B を結びつけて考える」という意味。ここでは、これが受身になっているだけ。いずれにせよ、使われる前置詞は with。A is associated with B の形で「A は B と関連がある」と覚えておいてもよい。

120. When the professor <u>made</u> two contradictory remarks, students began to
　　　　　　　　a　　　　　　b
　　　<u>the questions</u> the credibility <u>of her lecture</u>.
　　　　　　c　　　　　　　　　　　d

答：c（the questions → question）教授が2つの矛盾する発言をしたとき、学生たちは彼女の講義の信頼性を疑問視し始めた。

120．begin to
　begin は動名詞も to 不定詞も取れる動詞（List 6 参照）。ここではすでに to が与えられているので動詞の原形を補えばよい。question はふつう名詞として使われるが、「質問する、疑う」という意味の動詞にもなる。よって c を question にすればよい。

Directions: Questions 121-130 are incomplete sentences. Beneath each sentence, you will see four words or phrases, marked a, b, c, and d. Choose the **one** word or phrase that best completes the sentence.

121. Tom is one of the students who will benefit ------- Mrs. Taylor's generous donation to the university.

    a. very seriously in
    b. in amazing luck
    c. financially from
    d. everybody around him

122. Interactive toys are likely to replace the more important interaction ------- children and caring adults.

    a. beside
    b. regardless
    c. upon
    d. between

123. Family members of those still missing had to speak at an emotional news conference, expressing ------- their sadness and anger.

    a. the both
    b. both
    c. both of
    d. and both

124. The government is pushing universities to ride the globalization wave ------- .

    a. recruiting foreign teachers and foreign students being admitted
    b. from to recruit foreign teachers and to admit foreign students
    c. by recruiting foreign teachers and admitting foreign students
    d. recruits foreign teachers and admits foreign students

125. It is admirable that Karen wishes to solve all the problems ------- , but it might be better if she asked her teacher for help.

    a. self-conscious
    b. by herself
    c. in itself
    d. itself included

126. Mr. Mercury was very concerned ------- the whereabouts of his cat.

   a. to
   b. about
   c. along
   d. upon

127. We expect new factors, such as classes offered through the Internet, to be reflected in our annual best universities survey; for now, however, the same names continue ------- the top places.

   a. for dominating
   b. by domination
   c. to dominate
   d. dominate

128. The freezing point of water is 32 ------- Fahrenheit.

   a. of degree
   b. degrees
   c. centigrades in
   d. centigrade points in

129. ------- the director's initial fears concerning the graphic nature of some of his film's scenes, the ratings board gave the movie a lenient R rating without a single cut.

   a. Despite of
   b. Spite of
   c. Despite
   d. Spite

130. Teachers differed ------- they taught their subjects in class.

   a. tremendously in how competently
   b. the competence in how
   c. competently from how
   d. from the tremendous competence

解答 121: c 122: d 123: b 124: c 125: b 126: b 127: c 128: b 129: c 130: a

121. Tom is one of the students who will benefit ------- Mrs. Taylor's generous donation to the university.
 a. very seriously in
 b. in amazing luck
 c. financially from
 d. everybody around him

答：c　トムは、テーラー夫人からの大学への気前よい寄付によって、経済的に恩恵を被るであろう学生の1人である。

121．benefit from

benefitは他動詞としても自動詞としても機能する。他動詞の場合「～を益する、～のためになる」という意味だが、ここでは選択肢dのみが目的語の役割を果たし、他動詞benefitを可能にする。しかしこれでは、Tom is one of the students who will benefit everybody around himで文が完結してしまい、Mrs. Taylor's以下に話がつながらない。ということで、ここでのbenefitは「(～で、～から)利益を得る、得をする」という意味の自動詞ということになる。「～で、～から」という部分はfromやbyに導かれるフレーズによって追加される。特にbenefit fromのパターンはよく見られるもの。よって答はc。副詞financiallyがbenefitのすぐ後に来ているが、もともと自動詞のbenefitなのでfinanciallyで文を終わらせ、「経済的に恩恵を被る」とだけすることも可能。そこに「何から」という情報を付け加えると、この問題文の形ができあがる。

122. Interactive toys are likely to replace the more important interaction ------- children and caring adults.
 a. beside
 b. regardless
 c. upon
 d. between

答：d　インタラクティブなおもちゃが、より重要な、子供と世話を施す大人の間のふれ合いに取って代わりそうである。

122．between A and B

「子供(A)と世話を施す大人(B)の間」というのだからbetween A and Bのパターンが求められている。beside「～のそばに」、regardless「～とは関係なく」、upon「～の上に」はどれも意味の上からアウト。

123. Family members of those still missing had to speak at an emotional news conference, expressing ------- their sadness and anger.
   a. the both
   b. both
   c. both of
   d. and both

答：b　未だに行方不明である人達の家族は、感情いっぱいの記者会見で話をしなければならず、悲しみと怒りの両方を打ち明けた。

123．both A and B
　　both は the を取らないので、a はアウト。c の both of は必ず（限定された）1 つの複数名詞を取るが、ここでは A and B の形だから、これも候補から外れる。d は and が余分。よって答は b。

124. The government is pushing universities to ride the globalization wave ------- .
   a. recruiting foreign teachers and foreign students being admitted
   b. from to recruit foreign teachers and to admit foreign students
   c. by recruiting foreign teachers and admitting foreign students
   d. recruits foreign teachers and admits foreign students

答：c　政府は大学に、外国人教師を雇い、外国人学生を入学させることで、国際化の波に乗るよう働きかけている。

124．by
　　「外国人教師を雇い、外国人学生を入学させることによって」という修飾句が、空所の前にある「政府は大学に、国際化の波に乗るよう働きかけている」という文に後続する。「～によって」は、受動態でおなじみの前置詞 by。答は、by ＋動名詞の形を持つ c である。選択肢 a には by がないし、being admitted の使われ方もおかしい。b では前置詞 from の後に動名詞ではなく to 不定詞が来ている。d は独立した動詞句で、空所の前にある文と文法的なつながりがない。

125. It is admirable that Karen wishes to solve all the problems ------- , but it might be better if she asked her teacher for help.
   a. self-conscious
   b. by herself
   c. in itself
   d. itself included

答：b　すべての問題を自分自身で解決したいというのは賞賛に値するが、カレンは先生に助けを求めたほうがよいのかもしれない。

125．by oneself
「自分で、独力で」というのは、by oneself。選択肢 a の self-conscious は「自意識の強い、人前を気にする」という形容詞だが、空所は形容詞の入るべきところではない。c と d には itself があるが、問題文中にはこれが指すものが存在しない。よって b が答。

> 126. Mr. Mercury was very concerned ------- the whereabouts of his cat.
>   a. to
>   b. about
>   c. along
>   d. upon
>
> 答：b　マーキュリー氏は、彼の猫がどこにいるのかをとても気にしていた。

126．be concerned about
「～を気にかける、心配する」というときの表現。be worried about と同じ意味である。about の他に、for、over、at も文脈によっては可。また that 節が来ることもある。with を使うと「～に関係している、関心がある」という意味（Note 8 参照）。また、他動詞 concern 「～に関することである」というのが問題になることも。

> 127. We expect new factors, such as classes offered through the Internet, to be reflected in our annual best universities survey; for now, however, the same names continue ------- the top places.
>   a. for dominating
>   b. by domination
>   c. to dominate
>   d. dominate
>
> 答：c　我々は、インターネットで提供される授業というような新しい要素を、毎年のベスト・ユニバーシティ調査に加味していく予定である。しかし、現在のところ、同じ大学名が上位を独占し続けている。

127．continue to
問題 120 の begin 同様、continue も to 不定詞、動名詞の両方を取ることができる動詞。動名詞のみの選択肢はないので、c の to dominate を選ぶことは容易であろう。

128. The freezing point of water is 32 ------- Fahrenheit.
   a. of degree
   b. degrees
   c. centigrades in
   d. centigrade points in

答：b　水の氷点は、華氏32度である。

128．温度

　degree「〜度」は可算名詞なので、もちろん複数の場合は-sがつく。問題文にあるFahrenheitは「華氏」。選択肢cとdに見えるcentigradeは、摂氏（Celsius）である。32℃はthirty-two degrees centigradeと読む。これに平行した形であるthirty-two degrees Fahrenheit、すなわちbが答。

129. ------- the director's initial fears concerning the graphic nature of some of his film's scenes, the ratings board gave the movie a lenient R rating without a single cut.
   a. Despite of
   b. Spite of
   c. Despite
   d. Spite

答：c　監督は最初、自分の映画の数シーンの描写が生々しいので心配していたが、レーティング委員会は、1つのカットもなしに、その映画に寛大なRレーティングを与えた。

129．despite/in spite of

　「〜にも関わらず」という前置詞はdespiteで、同じ意味を持つ成句がin spite ofである。よって選択肢中正しいのはcのみ。

130. Teachers differed ------- they taught their subjects in class.
   a. tremendously in how competently
   b. the competence in how
   c. competently from how
   d. from the tremendous competence

答：a　教員は、どれくらいうまく担当科目をクラスで教えているかという点において千差万別であった。

130. differ

　この動詞は自動詞で、「異なる、違う」という意味を持つ。「～と」というときは、派生語 different と同様、from を取る。また、問題文にあるように「～という点において」というときは、in（または over、about、on 等）が出て来る。また、両方が同時に使われることもある。e.g. Ken differed from Mark in opinion.「ケンはマークと意見が違った。」さて、選択肢 b であるが、the competence が目的語の位置にある。これは differ が自動詞なのでおかしい。c では competently「有能に」が differ にかかるのが意味上変であるし、from「～と」が導くものが how they taught their subjects in class というのが決定的におかしい。d も同様で、「～と」にあたる部分が the tremendous competence「非常なる有能さ」というのは現実にはありえないし、また、文がここで終わってしまい、they 以下に続いていかない。よって答は a。

品詞と機能(2)

　さて、Note 5 では句動詞のことを説明したが、ここでその特徴を簡単に復習しておこう。make up などに見られるように、真の句動詞というのは、ふつう動詞と前置詞とから成り、Henry made up the incident と Henry made the incident up からわかるように、前置詞は目的語の後に移動可能である。また、目的語が代名詞の場合、この移動は必要不可欠になるので、Henry made it up はよいが、*Henry made up it はアウトである。

　しかしながら、ここに見られる up は副詞であり、それゆえ動詞句を修飾する「おまけ」であるとする向きがある。おまけなのだから、わざわざ動詞とセットにして句動詞という特別扱いをするまでもない、と議論は続く。このような分析は、特に動詞とそれに対応する句動詞の間にあまり意味の差がない場合、例えば、(3a) の tear「破る」に対し、(3b) の tear up「破りあげる」というような場合に多く見られる。

　(3) a. I tore the piece of paper.　　b. I tore the piece of paper up.

　とはいえ、この up を単なる副詞の修飾語とし、「句動詞とするまでもない」、と言ってしまうのは考え物である。これだと (3b) はともかく、下の (4a) が許されることの説明がつかない。副詞は通例、動詞と目的語の間に挟まれることはないからだ (*I tore quickly the paper ではなく、I quickly tore the paper か I tore the paper quickly としなければならない)。また、上に見た句動詞の特徴を無視することにもなる。(4a) では up が動詞と目的語の間に置かれてもよいが、(4c) ではだめで (4b) のようにしなければならない。これを説明するのに、目的語がふつうの名詞句か代名詞かということに言及するのなら、結局、句動詞の特徴を言っているのに他ならない。よって、up を副詞のおまけとする解釈は成り立たず、はっきり、句動詞と明言したほうがよいということになる。

　(4) a. I tore up the piece of paper.　　b. I tore it up.
　　　c. *I tore up it.

　また、up 自身にも品詞としての副詞の特徴など何もない。比較級もないし (upper は今では独立語)、最上級もない。very とも通例共起しない。一方、I tore it right up に見られるように、right を修飾語として取るが、これは前置詞の特徴の1つである。また、down the street に対する up the street は明らかに前置詞 up の用例。よって、up の品詞を副詞とするのには無理があり、句動詞においても、やはり、「副詞的な機能を持つ前置詞」としたほうが無難だということである。

Directions: In questions 131-140 each sentence has four underlined words or phrases. The four underlined parts of the sentence are marked a, b, c, and d. Identify the **one** underlined word or phrase that must be changed in order for the sentence to be correct.

131. In order to improve <u>efficiency,</u> we must find a solution <u>to</u> each major
                                      a   b
     <u>problems</u> <u>in</u> our company.
         c   d

132. I <u>had</u> <u>no idea</u> Karen and you were <u>that fond</u> of each <u>another.</u>
        a   b   c   d

133. <u>Neither</u> Hillary <u>nor</u> her friends <u>is</u> going to <u>class</u> today.
         a   b   c   d

134. She is a <u>very</u> <u>talented</u> actress <u>whom</u> you enjoy <u>to watch.</u>
             a   b   c   d

135. Politicians, professors, and <u>ugly</u> buildings <u>all</u> get <u>respectable</u> if they
                                 a   b   c
     last <u>enoughly long.</u>
             d

136. At their very <u>firstly</u> encounter, the banker
      a   b
     <u>deliberately mispronounced</u> the detective's name as a slight <u>put-down.</u>
             c   d

137. Our meetings always drone <u>on into</u> the night, crawling <u>with</u> one
                                         a   b
     excruciatingly minor administrative <u>detail</u> to <u>another.</u>
                                           c   d

138. <u>For</u> more than a year, Miss White has been trying to <u>make</u> her shy
       a   b
     students to <u>voice</u> their opinions <u>in class.</u>
                    c   d

139. This movie is not an indictment of the university system, but it does
                           a   b
    question the unchecked power that is given with people who may
       c   d
    abuse it.

140. The detective finally revealed to her that with well intentions, he had
                                         a   b
    tried to prevent something terrible from happening there to a woman
                                                          c
    he cared for, only to hasten the tragedy.
                      d

解答 131: c 132: d 133: c 134: d 135: d 136: b 137: b 138: b 139: d 140: b

---

131. In order to improve <u>efficiency</u>, we must find a solution to each major <u>problems</u>
　　　　　　　　　　　　　a　　　　　　　　　　　　　　　　　　b　　　　　　　　c
in our company.
d

答：c（problems → problem）能率を上げるために、我が社における大きな問題のそれぞれに対する解決策を見つけねばならない。

---

131. each/every

　　eachとeveryは文法上単数の名詞にしかつかない。よって下線cは単数のproblemでないとまずい。everybodyなどは（口語では）その意味から複数代名詞theyで受けることが多々あるが、これは文法的には誤りであるとされる（Note 9参照）。

---

132. I had <u>no</u> <u>idea</u> Karen and you were <u>that</u> fond of each <u>another</u>.
　　　　　　a　　b　　　　　　　　　　　　c　　　　　　　　d

答：d（another → other）カレンと君がそれほどお互いを気に入っているとはまったく知らなかった。

---

132. each other

　「お互い」という意味の表現。もう1つ同じ意味でone anotherがある。each otherとone anotherの違いについて、2人の間で「お互い」というときは前者、後者は3人以上の場合に使う、というルールを唱える人もあるが、実際にはあまり守られてはいないようだ。

---

133. <u>Neither</u> Hillary <u>nor</u> her friends <u>is</u> going to <u>class</u> today.
　　　　　a　　　　　　b　　　　　　　c　　　　　　d

答：c（is → are）ヒラリーも彼女の友達も、今日は授業に出ない。

---

133. neither A nor B

　「AもBも～ない」というこの成句が主語であるとき、動詞はBの名詞句との間に一致の現象を起こす。問題文ではher friendsがBにあたるので、動詞は複数のareが正解。同じルールがeither A or B「AかBのどちらか」にもあてはまる（Note 10参照）。

---

134. She is a <u>very</u> <u>talented</u> actress <u>whom</u> you enjoy <u>to watch</u>.
　　　　　　　a　　　b　　　　　　c　　　　　　　d

答：d（to watch → watching）彼女は見ていて楽しい、とても才能のある女優だ。

134. enjoy＋動名詞

enjoy は、to不定詞ではなく動名詞を取る動詞。他にも動名詞のみを取る動詞があるので、List 7 を確認して覚えておこう。

---

135. Politicians, professors, and <u>ugly</u> buildings <u>all</u> <u>get respectable</u> if they last
             a   b   c

<u>enoughly long</u>.
 d

答：d（enoughly long → long enough）政治家と大学教授と醜い建築物は、長くもてば、みんな尊敬の対象になる。

---

135. enough

enough は、形容詞と副詞を修飾する場合、常にその後に来る。名詞を修飾するときは、名詞の前に来るのがふつうであるが、forやto不定詞を伴うと、名詞の後に現れることも可能になる。e.g. There is beer enough for everybody.「みんなに充分なだけビールがある。」ちなみに、enoughly という形は存在しない。

---

136. At their very <u>firstly</u> encounter, the banker <u>deliberately mispronounced</u> the
   a   b   c

detective's name as a slight <u>put-down</u>.
          d

答：b（firstly → first）初めて会ったときに、銀行家は少し馬鹿にして探偵の名前をわざと間違えて発音した。

---

136. first vs. firstly

序数 first は、形容詞のように名詞を前から修飾するが、firstly は「第1に」という意味の副詞で、ふつう文頭に用いられる（firstが副詞として用いられる場合はこの限りではない）。ここでは、名詞 encounter を修飾するのだから、firstが正しい。

---

137. Our meetings always drone <u>on into</u> the night, crawling <u>with</u> one excruciatingly
           a   b

minor administrative <u>detail</u> <u>to another</u>.
        c   d

答：b（with → from）我々のミーティングは、苦痛なほどつまらない管理的詳細から詳細へとのろのろ進み、いつも夜まで続いてしまう。

---

137. from A to B

基本的なパターンである。前置詞 to は単独で使われることも多いが、to を見たら一応 from とのセットでないかと疑ってみるくせをつけておくとよい。

138. For more than a year, Miss White has been trying to make her shy students to voice their opinions in class.
　　　　　　　　　　　　　　　　　　　a　　　　　　　　　　b
　　　　　　　c　　　　　　　　d

答：b（make → get）ホワイト先生は、シャイな教え子たちにクラスで意見を言わせる努力を1年以上している。

138．get〜to

ここでのvoice は、「（意見などを）言う」という動詞。もし、使役動詞makeを使うのだったら、この動詞は原形でなくてはならない。しかし、ここではto voiceになっており、下線の引かれ方からして、原形に直すことはできない。そこでmakeを、同じように使役の意味を持つgetに換える。getは目的語の後にto不定詞を取るので、正しい文ができあがる。また、make同様に動詞の原形を取る使役動詞としてletとhaveも覚えておこう（問題165参照）。

139. This movie is not an indictment of the university system, but it does question
　　　　　　　　　　a　　　　　　　　　　　b　　　　　　　　　　　　　　c
the unchecked power that is given with people who may abuse it.
　　　　　　　　　　　　　　　　　d

答：d（with → to）この映画は大学システムの告発ではないが、乱用しかねない者に与えられる制限なしの権力についてはっきり疑問を投げかけている。

139．間接目的語

giveのような動詞はSVOOの文型を作り、2つの目的語は「間接目的語、直接目的語」の順番になっている。これは逆転も可能で、間接目的語がtoを伴って「直接目的語、to-間接目的語」となってもよい。さて、ここから受動態の文を作るのであるが、直接目的語を主語にする受動態文では、ふつう「直接目的語、to-間接目的語」の構文が反映され、間接目的語はtoを伴ったものになる。問題139では、関係節が受動態であり、その主語はもともと直接目的語であったthe unchecked power（あるいはそれを受ける関係代名詞that）であり、よって、後に残る間接目的語people who may abuse itにはwithではなくtoがつくのである。（ちなみに、過去分詞givenが形容詞的に使われた場合、それが修飾するのは直接目的語に相当するものである。given＋（to）間接目的語というパターンは存在しない。）

140. The detective finally revealed to her that with well intentions, he had tried to
　　　　　　　　　　　　　　　　　　　ａ　　　　　　　ｂ
　　prevent something terrible from happening there to a woman he cared for,
　　　　　　　　　　　　　　　　　　　　　ｃ
　　only to hasten the tragedy.
　　ｄ

答：b（well intentions → good intentions）よかれと思って、好きな女にひどいことが起こるのを防ごうと頑張ったのだが、結局悲劇を早めただけだったと、ついに探偵は彼女に明かした。

140. good vs. well
　goodは形容詞、wellは「健康な」という意味のときは形容詞として機能するが、ふつうはgoodの副詞形である。ここでは、「よい意図で」というのだから、やはり形容詞goodを使って名詞intentionsを修飾するのが正しい。

Directions: Questions 141-150 are incomplete sentences. Beneath each sentence, you will see four words or phrases, marked a, b, c, and d. Choose the **one** word or phrase that best completes the sentence.

141. I have no ------- what the speaker meant by the opening remark in his speech.

    a. knowledge
    b. thought
    c. idea
    d. willingness

142. It was while lying on her sofa that she first ------- about another patient whose story seemed larger than life.

    a. listened
    b. surprised
    c. considered
    d. heard

143. This is the approach that we recommend to help students ------- , academically and socially.

    a. gotten along with their classmates
    b. cope with growing demands
    c. in the need of theirselves
    d. the possible best way

144. No other city ------- has ever created a billboard environment quite like Kabukicho's.

    a. of world
    b. with world famous
    c. beyond worldwide
    d. in the world

145. Following the publication of his first paper in a major scientific journal, the researcher has seven other projects pending, ------- one about animal communication.

    a. including
    b. followed up
    c. to be continued
    d. which is

146. Students ------- advanced physics should come to see me.

   a. with interesting of
   b. are of interest to
   c. who are interested in
   d. earning big interest with

147. Jane was working 90 hours a week as a freelance technical writer, not because she needed the money but because ------- .

   a. she didn't know how to say no
   b. she was too afraid that lose her job
   c. her life was very bored
   d. she certainly knew to write novels

148. The climate here is ------- than that of California.

   a. at least mildless
   b. the least mildest
   c. less milder
   d. less mild

149. The new anti-crime law will fill prisons with criminals who are ------- dangerous than murderers.

   a. very lesser
   b. far less
   c. much lesser
   d. much too less

150. Both ------- intended to be famous.

   a. Jimmy, Eric, and Jeff
   b. Jimmy, and Eric, Jeff
   c. Jimmy, Eric, Jeff as well
   d. Jimmy and Eric, as well as Jeff,

解 答　141: c　142: d　143: b　144: d　145: a　146: c　147: a　148: d　149: b　150: d

141. I have no ------- what the speaker meant by the opening remark in his speech.
 a. knowledge
 b. thought
 c. idea
 d. willingness

答：c　演説者がスピーチの最初の発言で何が言いたかったのか、私には見当もつかない。

141．have no idea
「何か考えがある、…だと思う」というときには、have an idea …。have no idea …で「まったくわからない」。このようにhaveとideaがセットになる。非常によく使われる表現である。

142. It was while lying on her sofa that she first ------- about another patient whose story seemed larger than life.
 a. listened
 b. surprised
 c. considered
 d. heard

答：d　彼女が、まさかと思うような話を持つ他の患者について最初に聞いたのは、ソファに横たわっているときだった。

142．hear vs. listen
　listenは、音楽や演説など、耳を傾けて何かを聴くときに使う。ここでは漠然と「人についての話を聞いた」というのだからhearが適切。surpriseとconsiderはともに他動詞としての用法しかないので前置詞（about）なしで目的語を取るべき。よってdが答。hear about …「…について聞く」。

143. This is the approach that we recommend to help students ------- , academically and socially.
 a. gotten along with their classmates
 b. cope with growing demands
 c. in the need of theirselves
 d. the possible best way

答：b　学問の上でも社会においても増えてきている要求に学生たちがうまく対処する手助けとして、我々が勧めるアプローチはこれである。

102

143. help

「人が〜するのを助ける」というときには、help＋人＋動詞の原形という形を使う。動詞の原形はto不定詞でもよいが、原形のほうがより一般的。選択肢bのみ動詞の原形（cope）を持つので、これが答。ちなみに、cにあるtheirselvesはthemselvesの間違い。dはthe best way possible「考えられうる最良の方法」の語順であるべき。

144. No other city ------- has ever created a billboard environment quite like Kabukicho's.
　　a. of world
　　b. with world famous
　　c. beyond worldwide
　　d. in the world

答：d　世界のどの都市も、歌舞伎町のような宣伝看板の環境を生み出していない。

144. in the world

worldには通例theがつく。よって、theが含まれる選択肢dが答となる。他にも慣例的にtheを取る名詞があるので覚えておこう（List 8参照）。

145. Following the publication of his first paper in a major scientific journal, the researcher has seven other projects pending, ------- one about animal communication.
　　a. including
　　b. followed up
　　c. to be continued
　　d. which is

答：a　主要な科学ジャーナルに最初の論文を掲載したのに続き、その研究者は他に動物のコミュニケーションについてのプロジェクトを含む7つの未完成プロジェクトを抱えている。

145. including

「〜を含んで」というときの表現。bのfollowedは過去分詞なので、byを伴って受身にでもしないとone以下につながっていかない。cのto be continuedは、「次回に続く」という決まり文句。これもby等がないとここでは後に続かない。dのwhich isは、先行詞がseven other projects ...というのだから、複数のwhich areであるべき。しかし、その後にあるのがone about ...であるからこれは単数。よっていずれにせよ正しい文にはならない。

146. Students ------- advanced physics should come to see me.
　　a. with interesting of
　　b. are of interest to
　　c. who are interested in
　　d. earning big interest with

答：c　上級物理に興味のある学生は、私に会いに来ること。

146．interested in
　be interested in「〜に興味がある」という基本的な成句に関する問題。aでは、前置詞withの後に名詞でなく形容詞interestingがあり、それだけでもアウト。bは、Students are of interest to advanced physics「学生は、上級物理にとって興味のあるものだ（of interest = interesting）」というおかしな意味を作り出す上、その後のshould come ...という動詞句につながっていかない。dにすると「上級物理で大きな利息を稼いでいる学生」ということになり、やはり意味に無理がある。答はc。また、interestはもともと「興味を持たせる」という他動詞で、これが出題されることもある（Note 11参照）。

147. Jane was working 90 hours a week as a freelance technical writer, not because she needed the money but because ------- .
　　a. she didn't know how to say no
　　b. she was too afraid that lose her job
　　c. her life was very bored
　　d. she certainly knew to write novels

答：a　ジェーンは週に90時間フリーのテクニカル・ライターとして働いていたが、お金が必要だったからではなく、断り方を知らなかったからだ。

147．know how to
　knowは目的語の位置に（正式には）to不定詞を取ることができず、必ずhow toを取る。（これに対してlearnは両方可能。）よってdがまず消える。選択肢bは、so - thatの形かtoo - toの形にでもするべき。cではboredがおかしい。これだと「彼女の人生がとても退屈している」ことになる。現在分詞boringが正しい（問題60〜62およびNote 11参照）。答はa。

148. The climate here is ------- than that of California.
　　a. at least mildless
　　b. the least mildest
　　c. less milder
　　d. less mild

答：d　ここの気候は、カリフォルニアのそれより穏やかでない。

148. less
　less は形容詞、副詞について「より～でない」という比較級を構成するが、このとき形容詞、副詞は比較級ではなく、原級でなければならない。このことから選択肢cはアウト。また、問題文にthanがあるので必ず比較級がいるのに、選択肢a、bにはそれがない。ちなみにaのmildlessという単語は存在しない。bは最上級が2つもあり冗長だし、thanとも共起できない。

---

149. The new anti-crime law will fill prisons with criminals who are ------- dangerous than murderers.
　　a. very lesser
　　b. far less
　　c. much lesser
　　d. much too less

答：b　その新しい犯罪防止法は、殺人犯よりもずっと危険性の少ない犯罪者たちで刑務所をいっぱいにするであろう。

149．less vs. lesser
　lesser「（より）劣った、（より）小さい」は絶対比較級と言われ、thanとともに用いられることはない（また、thanの有無に関係なく、形容詞および副詞について「より～でない」という形を作ること自体ない）。この問題文にはthanがあるので、普通の比較級の文であることがわかる。よって、選択肢aとcの可能性はなくなる。比較級の意味を強めるのに、dにあるようなmuch tooは使われない。よってfarがless dangerousを強めているbが答。

---

150. Both ------- intended to be famous.
　　a. Jimmy, Eric, and Jeff
　　b. Jimmy, and Eric, Jeff
　　c. Jimmy, Eric, Jeff as well
　　d. Jimmy and Eric, as well as Jeff,

答：d　ジェフ同様ジミーとエリックも有名になるつもりだった。

150．成句の合作
　both A and Bは、基本的に2つのものをつなぐのに使われる（問題123参照）。よって、この成句のみで3つのものをつなごうとするa、bおよびcはすべてアウト（aに至ってはandすらもない）。正答dでは、both A and Bに、B as well as C「Cと同じくBも」という成句を組み合わせ、both A and B as well as Cの形を作り、3つのものが正しくつながれている、また、この形はdのようにカンマを伴うこともある。

Directions: In questions 151-160 each sentence has four underlined words or phrases. The four underlined parts of the sentence are marked a, b, c, and d. Identify the **one** underlined word or phrase that must be changed in order for the sentence to be correct.

151. The lawyer reached his conclusion on the <u>base</u> of a rumor that his
                                                                         a
     client had been forced to <u>pretend that</u> she <u>had indeed hired</u> a private
                                   b   c
     detective <u>for some reason</u>.
                    d

152. Miss White has been known <u>to give</u> wake-up calls to students who
                                             a
     are <u>chronically late</u> to school <u>so that</u> they get up and get there
                b   c
     <u>by time</u>.
      d

153. <u>Dozens</u> of old books <u>are stacked</u> <u>on top of</u> one <u>other</u> on his desk.
        a   b   c   d

154. One <u>on</u> three <u>flights last year</u> was cancelled, delayed, or diverted to
          a   b
     <u>another airport</u>; 173 million passengers <u>were affected</u>.
           c   d

155. The school that the juvenile delinquent <u>had been</u> sent to was <u>that of</u>
                                                      a   b
     13 reform schools that <u>received children</u> from <u>the D.C.</u> area.
                                       c   d

156. This is <u>a neighborhood</u> that <u>basically</u> deals with <u>own</u> problems
                a   b   c   d
     internally.

157. The international student advisor made a few only exceptions to the
                                        ─────── ────── ──────────   ──
                                           a   b   c
    rules regarding transferring credits from foreign universities.
    ──────────────────────────
                d

158. The father came out the retirement to assist his son, who had taken
                         ───   ──────   ─── ───
                          a   b   c   d
    over his business.

159. The teachers are trying very hard to persuade their least-motivated
    ─────────────── ─────────────   ──────────────
            a   b   c
    students for learning to be fun.
             ───────────────────────
                        d

160. The detective feared that his client might be planning on flee
                   ──────────   ──
                        a   b
    the scene with the crime's only witness.
    ─────────────   ─────────────────
          c   d

解　答　151: a　152: d　153: d　154: a　155: b　156: d　157: b　158: a　159: d　160: b

151. The lawyer reached his conclusion on the <u>base</u> of a rumor that his client had
　　　　　　　　　　　　　　　　　　　　　　　　　a
been forced to <u>pretend that</u> she <u>had indeed hired</u> a private detective
　　　　　　　　　　　b　　　　　　　　　　c
<u>for some reason.</u>
　　　d

答：a（base → basis）弁護士が結論を下したのは、何らかの理由で私立探偵を確かに雇ったというふりをするよう、彼の依頼人が強要されていたという噂に基づいてであった。

151. on the basis of
「〜に基づいて」というときの表現。base ではなく basis を使う。他に、on a regular basis「定期的に」、on a first-name basis「名前で呼び合う間柄で」等の表現も覚えておくとよい。

152. Miss White has been known <u>to give</u> wake-up calls to students who are
　　　　　　　　　　　　　　　　　　　　a
<u>chronically late</u> to school <u>so that</u> they get up and get there <u>by time.</u>
　　　b　　　　　　　　　　c　　　　　　　　　　　　　　　　d

答：d（by time → on time）ホワイト先生は、いつも遅刻する生徒たちにモーニング・コールをかけて彼らを起こし、時間通りに登校させることで知られている。

152. on time
「時間通りに」は、on time。「〜までに」という by を使うのであれば、by 8:30「8 時半までに」というように、具体的な時間を入れるとよい。

153. Dozens of <u>old books</u> <u>are stacked</u> <u>on top of</u> <u>one other</u> on his desk.
　　　　　　　　　a　　　　　　b　　　　　c　　　　d

答：d（other → another）何十冊もの古い本が、彼の机の上に積み重なっている。

153. one another
「本がお互いの上に積まれている」というのが直訳。one を使った「お互い」は one another である（問題 132 参照）。

154. One <u>on</u> three <u>flights last year</u> was cancelled, delayed, or diverted to
　　　　　 a　　　　　　 b
<u>another airport</u>; 173 million passengers <u>were affected</u>.
　　　c　　　　　　　　　　　　　　　d
答：a（on → in）昨年、3便に1便はキャンセルされたか、遅れたか、あるいは目的地以外の空港に変更され、1.73億人の乗客に影響が出た。

154．one in ...

「〜につき1つ」というときに使う前置詞は、onでなくin。似た表現にout ofを使ったものがある（問題12参照）。

155. The school that the juvenile delinquent <u>had been sent to</u> was <u>that of</u> 13 reform
　　　　　　　　　　　　　　　　　　　　　　 a　　　　　　　　 b
schools that <u>received children</u> from <u>the D.C. area</u>.
　　　　　　　　 c　　　　　　　　　　　 d
答：b（that → one）その不良が送られた学校は、ワシントン地区から子供を受け入れる13の少年院の1つであった。

155．one of ...

問題29で見たように、比べるものを同じにするときにthat ofの形がよく用いられるが、ここでは何も比べられていない。よって、下線部bがおかしいことがわかる。「不良が送られた学校は、13ある少年院の1つ」という解釈がもっとも妥当であろうから、thatの代わりにoneにするとよい。

156. This is a <u>neighborhood</u> that <u>basically</u> <u>deals with</u> <u>own</u> problems internally.
　　　　　　　　　　　 a　　　　　　 b　　　　 c　　　　 d
答：d（own → its own）ここは、自らの問題は基本的に内部で対処する地域である。

156．one's own

代名詞の格（問題25）のところですでに見た問題。「〜自身の」というownは、単独で使われることはなく、常に所有格（代）名詞を伴う。主語は、関係代名詞thatが受けるa neighborhoodだから、its ownが正しい形である。

157. The international student advisor made a few only exceptions to the rules
　　　　　　　　　　　　　　　　　　　　　a　　　b　　　　　　　　c
　　　regarding transferring credits from foreign universities.
　　　　　　　　　d

答：b (a few only → only a few) インターナショナル・スチューデント・アドバイザーは、外国大学からの単位振り替えに関する規則にごくわずかの例外しか認めなかった。

157．only a few

　基本的なことだが、few と little は、それぞれ可算名詞と不可算名詞について「ほとんどない」という意味を表し、「少しある」とするには、不定冠詞 a をつけて a few、a little にする。さて、ここで問題になっているのは、これらの意味の強め方。few および little であれば、very few、very little でよいが、a few と a little では only を用い、only a few、only a little とする。よって、下線部 b を only a few に直せばよい。

158. The father came out the retirement to assist his son, who had taken over his
　　　　　　　　　　　　　　a　　　　　　　b　　　　c　　　　　d
　　　business.

答：a (the → of) 父親は、すでに仕事を継いでいた息子を助けるために、隠居生活から復帰した。

158．out of ...

　「〜から」というのには、from か out of を使うのがふつう。ここでは「引退から出て来た」という直訳どおり out of が必要である。

159. The teachers are trying very hard to persuade their least-motivated students
　　　　　　　　　a　　　　　b　　　　　　　　　　　　　　　　　c
　　　for learning to be fun.
　　　　　　　d

答：d (for learning to be fun → that learning is fun) 教員たちは、学ぶことが楽しいことを最もやる気のない生徒たちに一生懸命悟らせる努力をしている。

159．persuade

　「説得する、確信させる」という persuade が取る構文はさまざま。ここでは、persuade A that 節で、「that 節の内容を A に確信させる」というもの。persuade A to 不定詞「A を〜するように説得する」の形はあるが、問題文のように for を含むものはない。

160. The detective feared that his client might be planning on flee the scene with
　　　　　　　　―――――――　　　　　　　　　　　　　　　―――　―――――――
　　　　　　　　　　a　　　　　　　　　　　　　　　　　　　　b　　　　c
the crime's only witness.
―――――――――――――――
　　　　　　d

答：b (on → to) 探偵は、依頼者がその犯罪の唯一の目撃者とともに現場を逃げるつもりなのかもしれないと危惧した。

160．plan to vs. plan on

　この2つの表現はともに「〜するつもりである」という意味を持つ。しかし、plan on を使うのなら、on が前置詞であるので動詞 flee「逃げる」は動名詞の fleeing でなければならない。ここでは、flee には下線がないので on を to にして plan＋to 不定詞の形にすればよい。

Directions: Questions 161-170 are incomplete sentences. Beneath each sentence, you will see four words or phrases, marked a, b, c, and d. Choose the **one** word or phrase that best completes the sentence.

161. -------, theoretical linguists look for principles in human language.

    a. Similar with biologists
    b. As same as physicians
    c. Such as chemists
    d. Like physicists

162. This letter is not interesting because -------.

    a. there is little news
    b. it does not offer many knowledges
    c. it is only about those few equipments
    d. of the writer repeats the same thing

163. For the hospital sequence, the movie director chose the Fairfield Hills Hospital, a facility ------- Newtown, Connecticut.

    a. to be managing in
    b. located in
    c. which situates themselves around
    d. which he was born

164. This gorgeous spring ------- the very cold winter.

    a. is up and running in
    b. certainly enjoys especially after
    c. is making up for
    d. has surely surprised us about a month ago

165. Dorothy is a very attractive woman with a wonderful sense of humor, and there is something about her ------- that she must be heaven-sent.

    a. which lets us imagining
    b. in which we are forced thinking
    c. where themselves are led to accept
    d. that makes you believe

166. ------- on radio and TV in Japan.

   a. There is much news programs
   b. There are many free language programs
   c. We have various news every day
   d. We hear numerous gossip daily

167. Although Takeo wanted to study in Indonesia, he ------- .

   a. didn't have much information about the country
   b. needed a large number of money to justify the cost
   c. was in need of many assistance in the Indonesian language
   d. had any friends that did not know him in Jakarta

168. Farmers' children ------- study at the institute because of the high tuition.

   a. do any longer afford to
   b. will not be allowed to longer
   c. may no longer be able to
   d. cannot longer

169. Child development experts suggest you play music for your child ------- for the purpose of building brain cells but for entertainment.

   a. only
   b. as
   c. especially
   d. not

170. One of the best reasons for taking this whiskey tasting class is that learning in a bar is not only expensive ------- .

   a. and yet too tempting
   b. but also difficult
   c. to everybody as well
   d. and also makes you drunk

解 答　161: d　162: a　163: b　164: c　165: d　166: b　167: a　168: c　169: d　170: b

161. ------- , theoretical linguists look for principles in human language.
    a. Similar with biologists
    b. As same as physicians
    c. Such as chemists
    d. Like physicists

答：d　物理学者と同様に、理論言語学者も人間言語内に原理を追い求める。

161. like

　　a にある similar は、with ではなく to と共起する。b における same は、the same as という形は取るが（問題 100 参照）、as same as という形は取らない。c の such as chemists「化学者のような」には、それが修飾するべき名詞が足りない。よって、答は d。問題 104 で見たように、like は前置詞で、前置詞句は形容詞的にも副詞的にも使われ得る。問題 161 は副詞的に使われている例である。また、like の派生形容詞 a like も副詞的に使われることがある。

162. This letter is not interesting because ------- .
    a. there is little news
    b. it does not offer many knowledges
    c. it is only about those few equipments
    d. of the writer repeats the same thing

答：a　この手紙は、ほとんどニュースがないのでおもしろくない。

162. little

　　b にある knowledge は不可算名詞なので複数形 knowledges など存在せず、可算名詞につく many と共起することもない。同様に、c の equipment も不可算名詞。複数形もなければ、可算名詞にのみつく few を取ることもない。d は、because of（of は前置詞）の後に節が来ているのでアウト。選択肢 a の little は、「～がほとんどない」という意味で、不可算名詞につく（問題 157 参照）。そして news は不可算名詞であるのでこれが答である。

163. For the hospital sequence, the movie director chose the Fairfield Hills Hospital, a facility ------- Newtown, Connecticut.
   a. to be managing in
   b. located in
   c. which situates themselves around
   d. which he was born

答：b　その映画監督は、病院の場面を撮るのにコネチカット州ニュータウンにある病院、フェアフィールド・ヒルズ病院を選んだ。

163．located

　もともとは be located in「〜にある」という形だが、過去分詞 located が形容詞的に用いられている（問題60参照）。本来 locate は他動詞で、「①（場所を）突き止める、②（場所に）〜を置く」という意味を持つが、ここでの located は②の用法が受身になったもの。また、文法的にはこの語がなくても正しい文が成り立つ (i.e. ... a facility (located) in Newtown, Connecticut)。選択肢 a は to 不定詞の形容詞的用法であるが、manage は他動詞なのに目的語がない。また、進行形なので、この動詞の意味上の主語が facility「施設」となることもおかしい。c では、themselves が何を指すのかわからないし、d では「彼（映画監督）が生まれたところ」というのだから、関係代名詞 which ではなく関係副詞 where が必要（問題74参照）。その上、Newtown, Connecticut にも前置詞がないと、この名詞句が宙に浮くことになってしまう。よって答は b。

164. This gorgeous spring ------- the very cold winter.
   a. is up and running in
   b. certainly enjoys especially after
   c. is making up for
   d. has surely surprised us about a month ago

答：c　今年のすばらしい春は、とても寒かった冬の埋め合わせになっている。

164．make up for

　a にある up and running というのは「大いに活動している」という意味で、これを選ぶとさっぱり訳のわからない文ができてしまう。b の enjoy は他動詞なので、目的語が必要だがそれがない。d は現在完了 (has surely surprised us) が過去の表現 (about a month ago) とともに使われている上（問題69参照）、the very cold winter にもつながっていかない。よって、答は c。make up for で「〜を補う、〜の埋め合わせをする」という意味。

165. Dorothy is a very attractive woman with a wonderful sense of humor, and there is something about her ------- that she must be heaven-sent.
　　a. which lets us imagining
　　b. in which we are forced thinking
　　c. where themselves are led to accept
　　d. that makes you believe

答：d　ドロシーはすばらしいユーモアのセンスを持った、とても魅力的な女性で、彼女には天与の人に違いないと思わせる何かがある。

165. 使役動詞
　使役動詞で押さえておくべきものは make、let、そして have である。これらはいずれも目的語の後に動詞の原形を取る。選択肢 a では let が使われているが、動詞の原形ではなく動名詞（imagining）が来ているので除外される。b で決定的におかしいのは forced thinking のところ。これは forced to think か forced into thinking であるべきだが、もしそうなっていたとしても意味の上ではじかれる。c では関係副詞 where がおかしいし、themselves も指すものがない。正答 d では、使役動詞 make が正しく使われている。

166. ------- on radio and TV in Japan.
　　a. There is much news programs
　　b. There are many free language programs
　　c. We have various news every day
　　d. We hear numerous gossip daily

答：b　日本には、ラジオとテレビの無料言語講座がたくさんある。

166. many
　これも基本をつく問題。many は可算名詞とのみ共起するので、選択肢 b の many free language programs が正しい形である。a は少しややこしいかもしれない。news は不可算名詞だが、news programs となると programs は数えられるので much ではなく many が必要。また動詞も are であるべき。c にある various（問題16参照）と d の numerous はともに可算名詞の複数形とのみ共起するので、news（不可算）や gossip（ふつう不可算；可算名詞としての用法もあるが、ここでは単数形になっている）と一緒ではおかしい。

167. Although Takeo wanted to study in Indonesia, he -------.
    a. didn't have much information about the country
    b. needed a large number of money to justify the cost
    c. was in need of many assistance in the Indonesian language
    d. had any friends that did not know him in Jakarta

答：a　タケオはインドネシアで勉強したかったが、その国について多くの情報を持ち合わせていなかった。

167．much

　　manyと対をなすmuchに関する問題。informationは不可算名詞で、不可算名詞のみにつくmuchと共起しているaが答である。bでは、可算名詞につくa (large) number ofが不可算のmoneyについているのでアウト（問題109参照）。cも同様に、可算名詞につくmanyが不可算のassistanceについているので除外される。dではany ... notという形が見て取れるが、これはnot ... anyの順番でなければならない。i.e. (he) did not have any friends that knew him in Jakarta.

168. Farmers' children ------- study at the institute because of the high tuition.
    a. do any longer afford to
    b. will not be allowed to longer
    c. may no longer be able to
    d. cannot longer

答：c　農民の子供は、授業料が高いので、もはやその学校で学ぶことはできないかもしれない。

168．no longer

　　no longerは、「もはや〜ない」という意味。これはふつう動詞の前に置かれる。この表現はnot ... any longerに書き換えられるが、この場合any longerは動詞句の最後のところに来る。つまり、Farmers' children may not be able to study at the institute any longerということ。これらのルールのいずれかにのっとっているのは、cのみ。

169. Child development experts suggest you play music for your child ------- for the purpose of building brain cells but for entertainment.
   a. only
   b. as
   c. especially
   d. not

答：d　幼児育成の専門家は、脳細胞を発達させる目的のためではなく、娯楽のために子供に音楽をかけてやるべきだと勧める。

169．not A but B

注意すれば、not for ... but for ... という並列の形が見て取れるであろう。not A but B で「A ではなく、B」という意味である。ここでも並列の形が保たれる（問題50～54参照）。

170. One of the best reasons for taking this whiskey tasting class is that learning in a bar is not only expensive ------- .
   a. and yet too tempting
   b. but also difficult
   c. to everybody as well
   d. and also makes you drunk

答：b　このウィスキーの利き酒クラスを取るべきもっともな理由の1つは、バーで学ぶのには金がかかるばかりでなく、難しいということである。

170．not only A but also B

受験英語でおなじみのパターン。よく also が省略された形も見られるが、TOEFL では、これを口語英語とみなし、also が伴われたもののみを正しい形とみなしている。答はもちろん b。

何のための留学？(1)

　ハーバード大学で一夏を過ごしたことがある。首都ワシントンにあるジョージタウン大学で博士課程の勉強を始めるにあたり、コースワークを早く終わらせたかったので、夏の間に取れる単位は取ってDCへ向かおうと思ったからだ。この計画はきちんと実行したが、ハーバードでの2ヶ月はあまり楽しいものではなかった。

　天下のハーバード大学である。どれほど優秀な人たちが集まっていて、どんな刺激を受けることができるのだろう、と大きな期待を持って大学に着いた。しかし、そこで待っていたのは、外国人用の英語コースに高い授業料を払って遊びに来ている遊学生たちだった。そしてその半分ほどが日本人。日本人の中で大学院の単位を取得しに来ていたのは私くらい。正規のハーバードの学生たちは、夏休みでみんな留守だった。

　ハーバード滞在中は、大学の寮に住んだ。幸か不幸か、私にはルームメートがいた。カリフォルニアからサンスクリット語を学びに来ていた堅物のおじさんで、数少ないアメリカ人の1人だった。お互いに自己紹介を兼ねて30分くらい話した後、一緒に寮の説明会に出た。バイトで寮長を務めるハーバードの学生がいろいろ説明してくれたが、ほとんどの日本人にはわからない。寮長が困っていると、私のルームメートが「こいつは日本人だが英語ができるから、通訳をさせたら？」という提案をした。寮長は喜んで、「何かあったら、彼に聞くように」と言って説明会を終えてしまった。

　というわけで、数人の日本人と話をすることになったが、まったく長続きすることはなかった。大体、寮のルールといっても、緊急時にはどこそこに連絡するように、というくらいのもので、その夏には緊急時など一切なかったし、彼らとは、授業を受けるスケジュールも教室もすべて違っていたからだ。しかし、同じ寮だから、挨拶くらいはする。みんな、アメリカで真の英会話力をつけるんだ、と言っていた。「では、練習のためにこれからは日本人同士でも英語を使ったほうがいいですね」と私が言うと、黙ってしまう人が多かった。

　確かに、日本人同士で英語を話すというのは、気恥ずかしい。しかし、彼らはいつも日本人と一緒なのだから、そうでもしないと何のためにアメリカに来たのかがわからない。実際、彼らは朝起きると同じ寮の日本人と一緒にカフェテリアに行き、日本語をしゃべる。授業にも一緒に行くのだが、この授業というのもアメリカの中の日本というべきもので、先生こそアメリカ人だが、クラスの15人中14人までが日本人であったりする。放課後も一緒にボストンへ行き、日本語をしゃべりまくって夜遊びをする。これでは、観光旅行と何の差もないではないか。本当に何のためにアメリカに来たのだろう？

(p.133に続く)

Directions: In questions 171-180 each sentence has four underlined words or phrases. The four underlined parts of the sentence are marked a, b, c, and d. Identify the **one** underlined word or phrase that must be changed in order for the sentence to be correct.

171. The mother <u>wanted to attribute</u> her child's bad mood <u>to</u> a lack of
                               a   b
     sleep <u>rather</u> to his <u>moody</u> disposition.
            c   d

172. Those laws <u>regardless</u> sanitation <u>are very</u> unpopular <u>with</u> janitors.
           a   b   c   d

173. I <u>think our</u> company <u>should</u> relocate <u>at</u> <u>a new</u> city.
          a   b   c d

174. The principal said she <u>would</u> allow class representatives to <u>service</u> <u>as</u>
                          a   b c
     <u>advisers</u> to the faculty meeting.
         d

175. Even <u>the nearest</u> hospital is several <u>mile away</u>.
           a   b   c   d

176. Mr. May's lesson <u>was something</u> <u>that</u> should <u>have to been</u>
                                   a   b   c
     remembered by <u>all his</u> followers.
                      d

177. <u>The attorney general's</u> recent comments about dealing with gun
                  a
     violence did not show <u>promising</u> <u>of</u> a good beginning for the
                                  b   c
     administration <u>on</u> this issue.
                    d

178. The problems of urban schools in the U.S. are too great that they
                  ─   ─────────   ───
                  a   b   c
    require firm decisions by people with financial and political clout.
                                    ──────────────────────────────────
                                                    d

179. In 1995, the guitar company altered its logo in that "Ray Vaughn"
                                 ─────────── ──
                                      a   b
    would appear in larger letters.
    ─────────────── ──
           c   d

180. The professor let us cost time in his office in order to get to know us
                   ─── ────   ──────────────────
                    a   b   c
    better.
    ──────
      d

解　答	171: c　172: b　173: c　174: b　175: c　176: c　177: b　178: c　179: b　180: b

171. The mother <u>wanted to attribute</u> her child's bad mood <u>to a lack of sleep</u> <u>rather</u>
　　　　　　　　　　a　　　　　　　　　　　　　　　　　b　　　　　　　　c
　　to his <u>moody disposition</u>.
　　　　　　　　d

答：c（rather → rather than）母親は、我が子の不機嫌を彼の気分屋の性格というよりも睡眠不足のせいにしたがった。

171．rather than

　A rather than B で「BよりもむしろA」という意味。AとBには並列の関係が保たれる。ratherのみで使われるときは「いくぶん、かなり」といった意味の副詞で、直後におかれる形容詞等を修飾する。e.g. We are rather tired.「私たちはかなり疲れた。」問題文では、to a lack of sleep と to his moody disposition が rather than で結ばれる形になっている。

172. Those laws <u>regardless</u> sanitation <u>are</u> very unpopular with <u>janitors</u>.
　　　　　　a　　　　　b　　　　　　　c　　　　　　　　　　　d
答：b（regardless → regarding）公衆衛生についてのその法律は、管理人たちにはとても不評である。

172．regarding

　regardless は単独で名詞を取ることはなく、of を伴って「～とは関係なく」という成句を構成する。これに対して、regarding は「～に関して(の)、～について(の)」という前置詞であるから、常に名詞を取る。意味の上から考えて regardless に of を加えるよりも、regardless を regarding に書き換えるべき。ちなみに、concerning も regarding と同じ意味を持つ前置詞。

173. I think our company should relocate at a new city.
　　　　　　　a　　　　　　　　　b　　　　c　d
答：c（at → to）我々の会社は、新しい都市に移転するべきだと思う。

173．relocate

　relocate には、他動詞と自動詞の両方があるが、自動詞として使われるケースが問題になっている。「～へ移転する」というのだから必要とされる前置詞は to。文脈によっては、違う前置詞が使われることがあるが、意味をよく考えれば難しくはない。e.g. Our company is relocating outside Tokyo.「うちの会社は東京の外に移転することになっている。」

174. The principal said she would allow class representatives to service as advisers
　　　　　　　　　　　　　　　　ａ　　　　　　　　　　　　　　　　　　　　　ｂ　　　　ｃ
　　 to the faculty meeting.
　　 ─
　　 ｄ
答：b（service → serve）校長は、学級委員たちが職員会議の顧問になることを許すと言った。

174．serve
　serviceはふつう名詞だが、「(～の) 手入れ・修理をする、(ガスなどを) 供給する」という意味の他動詞としても働くこともある (自動詞はない)。しかし、問題文ではserviceに目的語がないし、意味の上からもこの動詞はおかしい。「(～として) 仕える、勤める」という意味を持つserveに換えるべき。(serve time「服役する」、serve a sentence「刑に服す」という表現も覚えておくとよい。)

175. Even the nearest hospital is several mile away.
　　　　ａ　　　　ｂ　　　　　　　　　　ｃ　　　ｄ
答：c（mile → miles）一番近い病院でさえ、数マイル離れている。

175．several
　この単語も可算名詞の複数形とともに用いられる (問題15、16、166参照)。よって、cのmileをmilesに直す。

176. Mr. May's lesson was something that should have to been remembered by
　　　　　　　　　　　　　　　　　　ａ　　　　　　　ｂ　　　　　　ｃ
　　 all his followers.
　　 ─
　　 ｄ
答：c（have to been → have been）メイ氏の教訓は、彼の信奉者みんなが覚えておくべきだった。

176．should have＋過去分詞
　「～するべきだった」と、しなかったことを後から悔やむ言い方である (つまり、仮定法過去完了：問題32参照)。下線部cにあるtoはto不定詞のそれであろうから、動詞の原形が後続しなければならない。しかし、過去分詞のbeenが来ているので、ここが誤りであることがわかる。toを消去すれば、「覚えておかれるべきであった」という正しい受身の構造ができる。ちなみに、must have＋過去分詞の形になると、「～したに違いない」という意味 (問題69、86参照)。

177. The attorney general's recent comments about dealing with gun violence did
       ―――――――――――――――
              a
   not show promising of a good beginning for the administration on this issue.
            ――――――― ――   ――――――――――――――
                b   c   d

答：b（promising → promise）拳銃暴力の対処に関する司法長官の最近のコメントは、政府にとってこの問題に関するよいスタートを予見するものではなかった。

177. show promise of

「～の見込み、きざしを示す」というこの成句では、promise が何の冠詞も伴わずに使われる。もちろん、問題文にあるような動名詞もアウト。よってbが答である。

178. The problems of urban schools in the U.S. are too great that they require firm
                 ―― ―――――――   ―――
                  a   b   c
    decisions by people with financial and political clout.
                        ――――――――――――――――――――――
                                    d

答：c（too → so）アメリカにおける都会の学校の問題はとてもひどいので、財政的そして政治的影響力を持つ人々によるしっかりした決断が必要である。

178. so ~ that

so ~ that ...「とても～なので…だ」というパターン。「～」の位置には形容詞か副詞が来る。too が関わるのは、too ~ to ...「あまりに～なので…できない」というもの。よって下線部cのtoo がso に換えられるべき。

179. In 1995, the guitar company altered its logo in that "Ray Vaughn"
                                ――――――――――― ――
                                      a   b
    would appear in larger letters.
    ―――――――――― ――
         c   d

答：b（in → so）1995年にそのギター会社は、「レイ・ボーン」の文字がより大きく表示されるように会社のロゴを変えた。

179. so that

A so that Bで、「BになるようにA」というもの。この問題文に見られる in that は「～という点において」という意味で、文脈に沿わない。よって下線部bのinをsoに換える。

180. The professor let us cost time in his office in order to get to know us better.
　　　　　　　　　　　ａ　　ｂ　　　　　　　　　　　　　　　　ｃ　　　　　ｄ

答：b（cost → spend）教授は、我々のことをよりよく知ろうと、彼の研究室を使わせてくれた。

180. spend time
　time は spend するもの。直訳すると「我々に研究室で時間を過ごさせてくれた」である。cost は、お金のように「支払うべきもの」を目的語に取る。よって、cost time という言い方は「～（するの）は時間の代償がいる」という意味で、その主語は人ではなく、ふつう事柄（もの）。問題文では、us が cost の意味上の主語であるから、これが誤りであることがわかる。ちなみに cost には、cost＋O1（人）＋O2（もの）「O1（人）に O2（損失など）を負担させる」という SVOO の文型もあるが、やはり主語は事柄（もの）。

Directions: Questions 181-190 are incomplete sentences. Beneath each sentence, you will see four words or phrases, marked a, b, c, and d. Choose the **one** word or phrase that best completes the sentence.

181. We expect the building to be finished -------.

    a. in three weeks future
    b. by nearly next week
    c. within the next two weeks
    d. in the near four weeks

182. The timid speaker was intimidated by ------- in the crowd.

    a. the thousands of faces
    b. thousand of people
    c. ten thousands of faces
    d. ten thousands people

183. An unidentified source said the civilians at the controls were under close supervision, and their presence ------- the accident.

    a. had a relationship of
    b. in relation to
    c. is relatively unknown with
    d. was unrelated to

184. The detective drove ------- the long, expansive driveway to the Mercury mansion.

    a. along with
    b. upward
    c. toward out of
    d. up

185. The actress ------- running around in very high, spiked heels.

    a. used to
    b. had to use to
    c. had to get used to
    d. had to get used to be

186. Humility may be ------- us in addressing the question of how to prevent misuse of genetic information as it becomes more available.

   a. more useful for
   b. used upward as
   c. used to make
   d. of some use up

187. Mario wishes ------- enough time to complete his homework before 3 o'clock.

   a. to have had to
   b. he must have had
   c. that he has
   d. that he had

188. Acting is like dancing ------- someone who is a really good dancer.

   a. together
   b. along together
   c. all night
   d. with

189. I ------- to another school than attend that stupid class.

   a. would rather to transfer
   b. would rather transfer
   c. will transfer rather
   d. will rather have to transferring

190. I love shopping; I would rather ------- until midnight.

   a. stores are open
   b. stores opening
   c. that stores stayed open
   d. that stores keep opening

| 解 答 | 181: c　182: a　183: d　184: d　185: c　186: a　187: d　188: d　189: b　190: c |

181. We expect the building to be finished ------- .
　　　a. in three weeks future
　　　b. by nearly next week
　　　c. within the next two weeks
　　　d. in the near four weeks

答：c　その建物は、ここ2週間以内に完成するだろうと我々は思っている。

181．the next/coming
　　未来の時間を表す場合「これから何日（何週、何年、etc.）」というのを強調するのに、the next ...あるいはthe coming ...という表現を使う。near「近い」やnearly「ほとんど」などは使わない。選択肢 a は、future がなければ「3週間で」という意味になり OK。答は c である。

182. The timid speaker was intimidated by ------- in the crowd.
　　　a. the thousands of faces
　　　b. thousand of people
　　　c. ten thousands of faces
　　　d. ten thousands people

答：a　臆病な演説者は、何千もの聴衆の顔を見ておびえてしまった。

182．thousands of
　　問題47で見たように、単に特定の数字、例えば2,000、というときは two thousand で、決して複数形の two thousands にはならないが、「何千もの」というときは、複数形を使って thousands of となる。よって b と d はアウト。また、位を上げて「何万もの」というときには、tens of thousands of、「何十万もの」なら hundreds of thousands of である。よって c も除外される。また、この問題文では、限定された聴衆の「何千もの顔」であるから、thousands of faces に定冠詞 the がついている。

183. An unidentified source said the civilians at the controls were under close supervision, and their presence ------- the accident.
　　　a. had a relationship of
　　　b. in relation to
　　　c. is relatively unknown with
　　　d. was unrelated to

答：d　未確認筋によると、操縦していた一般人たちは厳重な監督下にあり、彼らの存在は事故とは無縁だということであった。

128

183．(un)related to

　related to で「〜と関連がある、〜と親戚である」という意味。その否定の形 unrelated to「〜と無関係で」も、やはり同じ前置詞 to を取るが、これは、もともと動詞 relate が to を取ることに起因する。選択肢 a にある relationship を使って「〜との関係」というのなら、前置詞は with（または to）。c のunknown も with ではなく to を取る。b の in relation to は「〜に関して、〜と比較して」という成句であるが、空所が求めるのは動詞句なのでここではアウト。よって、答はd。

184．The detective drove ------- the long, expansive driveway to the Mercury mansion.
　　a. along with
　　b. upward
　　c. toward out of
　　d. up

答：d　探偵の車は、マーキュリー大邸宅の長く、広々した車道を登っていった。

184．up vs. upward

　up は前置詞なので、後に名詞句を取るが、upward「上のほうへ」は副詞なので単独で使われる。空所の後には名詞句 the long, expansive driveway to the Mercury mansion「マーキュリー邸へと続く長くて広々とした（邸内の）車道」があるので、b はアウト。a の along with「〜と一緒に」は、意味の上で除外される。また、c の toward out of という組み合わせは存在しない。よって答は d。

185．The actress ------- running around in very high, spiked heels.
　　a. used to
　　b. had to use to
　　c. had to get used to
　　d. had to get used to be

答：c　女優は、先細のとても高いヒール靴を履いて走り回るのに慣れなければならなかった。

185．be/get used to

　「〜に慣れている／慣れる」というこの成句中の to は前置詞なので、後には名詞、動名詞が来る。これに対して、used to「（かつて）〜した」の to は to 不定詞のそれなので、動詞の原形が後続する。選択肢 a を選ぶと、used to ＋動名詞になるのでアウト。b の use to という形は存在しない。d では get used to の後に動詞の原形が来ているのでやはり適切でない。答は c。

186. Humility may be ------- us in addressing the question of how to prevent misuse of genetic information as it becomes more available.
 a. more useful for
 b. used upward as
 c. used to make
 d. of some use up

答：a　遺伝情報が得られるにつれ、その誤用をいかに防ぐかという問題に対処するのに、謙虚さが我々にとってより有用になるのかも知れない。

186．useful for
　　まず、bのused upward asだが、こういうコンビネーションはない。選択肢cは、空所の直前のbeと一緒になってbe used to「～に慣れている」を作るが、主語がhumility「謙虚さ、謙遜」であり意味がおかしくなる上、前置詞toの後に動詞の原形makeが来ているので、文法的にもアウト（問題185参照）。dのof some useはtoを伴っていれば「～に少し役立つ」という成句になるのだが、upなのでやはり除外される。答はa。usefulはforまたはtoを伴い「（人）に役立つ」という意味になる。(forは「～するのに」というときにも使われる。)「～において」というには、この問題文にあるようにinを使うのがふつう。

187. Mario wishes ------- enough time to complete his homework before 3 o'clock.
 a. to have had to
 b. he must have had
 c. that he has
 d. that he had

答：d　マリオは、もっと時間があって3時前に宿題を終わらせられたらなあ、と思っている。

187．wish
　　この動詞が取るthat節は必ず仮定法となる。言い換えれば、wishは仮の話とせざるを得ないこと（つまり、ありえないこと）を望むのに使う動詞であるということ。e.g. I wish I were a bird.「僕は鳥だったらなあ。」現在の状況に反することを望むのなら（仮定法）過去を使い、過去に起きてしまったことの仮定なら（仮定法）過去完了である。さて、問題187であるが、選択肢cでは動詞が現在形なのでアウト。bのmust have＋過去分詞の形は「～したに違いない」という意味で（問題176参照）、ここでは意味が通らないし、仮定法でもないので候補から外れる。また、wishはto不定詞も取るが、aにおけるto have had toは、意味もおかしいし、to不定詞に動詞の原形ではなくenoughが後続することになるので除外。答は仮定法過去のd。

188. Acting is like dancing ------- someone who is a really good dancer.
   a. together
   b. along together
   c. all night
   d. with

答：d　演技とは、本当にダンスのうまい人と踊るようなものである。

188．with vs. together
　withは前置詞だが、togetherは副詞。ちょうど問題184と同じように、前者は名詞句を取るが、後者は単独で使われるというパターン。よって、選択肢aのtogetherは、someone以下の名詞句を取らないのでアウト。bのalong togetherという組み合わせはない（along withについては問題113参照）。cのall night「一晩中」も副詞として機能し、やはりsomeone以下が続かなくなる。答は前置詞のwith。

189. I ------- to another school than attend that stupid class.
   a. would rather to transfer
   b. would rather transfer
   c. will transfer rather
   d. will rather have to transferring

答：b　あの馬鹿らしい授業に出るよりも転校したほうがましだ。

189．would rather (1)
　would rather A than B「BよりはむしろA」のwould ratherはhad better同様、2語で1つの助動詞のように振舞う。すなわち、直後には動詞の原形を取り（e.g. would rather transfer、had better transfer)、否定の形も直後にnotを従える（e.g. would rather not transfer、had better not transfer)。選択肢aではwould ratherの後にto不定詞が来ているのでアウト。cとdでは、wouldがwillになっているし、cは語順もおかしい。また、dのhave to transferringは、have to＋動詞の原形というルールを無視している。

190. I love shopping; I would rather ------- until midnight.
　　a. stores are open
　　b. stores opening
　　c. that stores stayed open
　　d. that stores keep opening

答：c　私はショッピングに目がない。午前0時まで店が開いていてほしいのだが。

190．would rather (2)
　would ratherはthat節を取ることもあるが、その場合that節内は仮定法。a、b、dはともに仮定法ではないので候補から消える。cのstayed openのみが仮定法（過去）であり、これが答（問題187参照）。

何のための留学？(2)

　本場アメリカまで英会話の修行に来て、日本語ばかり話して生活するというのは、私には考えられないことだ。私はハーバードへ行く直前まで、アメリカの大学の日校で英語を教え、つい日本語で話してしまう学生たちに、Speak English!　と言うのが日課だった。いくら、かっこいい英語教育論を唱えても、教師である私が身を持ってすべてのことを英語でこなす姿を見せなくては示しがつかない。同僚のほとんどがアメリカ人だったので、教室の内外を問わず英語のみを話して過ごした。学生とハイキングや野球観戦に行くときも英語しか話さなかった。学生から電話をもらっても英語で通した。そうこうするうちに学生たちも恥ずかしがらずに英語を使うようになり、TOEFLの点も伸びてアメリカの本校へ旅立つ者が出てきた。その後アメリカでがんばる彼らから、ワシントンのアパートで英語の電話を受けたときは、とても嬉しかった。

　こういう背景のある私である。どうして、日本語しか話さない日本人グループに入れよう。よって、すぐ（特別な場合を除いて）日本語を一切話さないようにした。数少ないアメリカ人を求め、授業の後も教授について回ったり、興味などないのに、自己暗示セミナーやヨガ教室に通った。そこではボストンのアメリカ人と議論や運動ができて楽しかった。また、同じ寮にロシア語を学びにオハイオから来ていた高校の歴史教員がいた。非常に勤勉な彼は、真のスポーツマンでもあり、つまらないハーバードの夏も、彼との出会いだけは期待以上のものであった。お互い勉強が忙しかったが、一緒にジョギングや水泳を楽しんだ。週末には、レッドソックスの試合を観に行ったりもした。真に心を開いて話をし、一生続く友情を育んだ。その２年後、彼のオハイオの家を訪れる機会を得たが、1999年の秋には、彼が私のところに来てくれた。

　それにしても、日本人は徒党を組んで、自分たちと違う者を揶揄するのが好きである。日本語（とスペイン語）しか聞こえてこないカフェテリアで、私は日本人グループの話題になっていたらしい。英語しか話さないが日本人のように見える。話しかける勇気はないから、食事中に背後から近づき、「肩に虫がとまっている！」と叫んでみて、振り向いたら日本人、そうでなければ外国人。こういういたずらを企んでいると、恋の相談に来た一匹狼の日本の女の子が教えてくれた。東欧からの留学生にぞっこんの彼女は、日本人グループに馴染めず、同じ一匹狼である私のところに来たということか。いずれにせよ、彼女とも２回しか話はしなかったが。

　期間の限られた留学で、なぜ、日本人グループなのか。これは、語学留学に限った問題では決してない。考えさせられる他の逸話や誤った留学神話は、またの機会にするが、皆さんも出発前にもう１度、ご自分の目標とやる気を確認されるとよいかも知れない。

Directions: In questions 191-200 each sentence has four underlined words or phrases. The four underlined parts of the sentence are marked a, b, c, and d. Identify the **one** underlined word or phrase that must be changed in order for the sentence to be correct.

191. If you want a statistical report on universities in the U.S., you should
                   a   b
    look for special editions of magazines as such *Newsweek* and *U.S.*
         c   d
    News and World Report.

192. The fact that one woman's passion could have such a positive effect
                                           a
    that this on so many people around her is amazing.
        b   c   d

193. In responsive to written questions from the committee this week, an
         a   b
    attorney for Candy Loving indicated she had given an "enormous
           c   d
    sum of money" to her lover's library.

194. It is often said that the musician Clive Davis has so a big ego that he
           a   b c
    thinks CD's were named after him.
                        d

195. We have taken special caring to see that the new toy will contain
                      a   b   c
    no dangerous parts.
         d

196. I was completely taken to surprise when the supervisor came to
                 a   b   c
    observe my class.
        d

197. No matter how beautifully my cake looks, it has to taste good,
           a   b   c
    or I'm not a good pastry cook.
       d

198. Concerned parties complained what this horror film should not have
          a   b
    been made available to minors, even if accompanied by their parents.
          c   d

199. The develop of a new teaching method requires much research.
       a   b   c   d

200. The high up we go, the colder it becomes.
        a   b c   d

> **解 答** 191: d 192: b 193: a 194: c 195: a 196: b 197: b 198: b 199: b 200: a

> 191. If you want a statistical report on universities in the U.S., you should look for
>   a   b   c
>   special editions of magazines as such *Newsweek* and *U.S. News and World*
>   d
>   *Report*.

答：d (as such → such as) アメリカの大学に関する統計的レポートがほしいなら、ニューズウィークおよびU.S.ニュース・アンド・ワールド・レポートのような雑誌の特集号を探すとよい。

191. such as(1)

　such as は前置詞 like と同様、「～のような、～といった」という意味（問題161参照）を持つ。as such は「そういうものとして、それ自体では」という独立した副詞的フレーズ。ここでは「ニューズウィークおよびU.S.ニュース・アンド・ワールド・レポートのような雑誌」というのだから such as が適当。

> 192. The fact that one woman's passion could have such a positive effect that this
>   a   b
>   on so many people around her is amazing.
>   c   d

答：b (that → as) 1人の女性の情熱が、周りにいるとても多くの人にこのようなポジティブな影響を与えられたとは驚きだ。

192. such as(2)

　such a positive effect as this で、「このようなポジティブな影響」ということ。このように such と as の間に名詞句が来ることもある。such - that というパターンもあるが、この場合 that 以下には節（つまりＳ＋Ｖの形）が必要（問題194参照）。仮に b の that が正しい形だとすると、それに続く節は this on so many people around her is amazing となるが、主節の主語であるべき The fact を主要部とする名詞句が動詞を伴わず、宙に浮いた形になってしまう。よって、下線部 b を as に直すべき。

193. In responsive to written questions from the committee this week, an attorney
       ─────────   ──
         a   b
    for Candy Loving indicated she had given an "enormous sum of money" to
    ─────────────────   ─────────
           c   d
    her lover's library.

答：a（responsive → response）委員会から今週寄せられた書面による質問に応じて、キャンディ・ラビングの弁護士は、彼女が愛人の図書館に「多額の金銭」を寄付していたことを明らかにした。

193．in response to

「～に応じて」という成句。responsive は「～に敏感な、～によく反応する」といった意味の形容詞。be responsive to の形でよく使われる。しかし、ここでは前置詞 in があるので、形容詞ではなく名詞の response が来るのが理にかなっている。

---

194. It is often said that the musician Clive Davis has so a big ego that he thinks
        ─────────────   ── ─
              a   b c
     CD's were named after him.
                    ──────────
                        d

答：c（so → such）よく言われることだが、ミュージシャンであるクライブ・デイビスはうぬぼれがとても強く、CD は自分の名にちなんでつけられたと思っている。

194．such ~ that

問題178の so - that と基本的には同じ。such A that B「とても A なので B」という構文である。so ではなく such が使われる理由は、A の位置に（形容詞に修飾された）名詞句が来ることである（問題文では a big ego「大きな自負心」が来ている）。so は形容詞（または副詞）のみを修飾するので、ここでは不適切。

---

195. We have taken special caring to see that the new toy will contain
                           ────── ──   ────────────
                             a   b   c
     no dangerous parts.
     ──────────────────
             d

答：a（caring → care）その新しいおもちゃに危険な部品が使われないよう、我々は特別な注意を払った。

195．take care

take care of「～の世話をする」からわかるように、この care は名詞で文法上 take の目的語である。take care ＋ to 不定詞は、「～するように気をつける、注意する」という意味の成句。よって下線部 a の動名詞 caring は care に直されるべき。

196. I was completely taken to surprise when the supervisor came to
    _____ _____ _____
            a   b   c
   observe my class.
   _____
          d

答：b (to → by) スーパーバイザーが私の授業を見に来たとき、私は完全に不意をつかれた。

196．take ～ by surprise
「～の不意をつく、～を驚かす」という意味の成句。ここでは、これが受動態で使われている。下線bのtoはbyであるべき。

---

197. No matter how beautifully my cake looks, it has to taste good, or I'm not a
    _____ _____   ____ _____
           a   b   c   d
   good pastry cook.

答：b (beautifully → beautiful) 私のケーキがどんなに美しく見えても、おいしくなければならない。でないと、私はよい菓子職人でないことになる。

197．五感の動詞
この文にあるlook「見える」とtaste「味がする」はいわゆる五感の動詞である。これらの動詞は副詞でなく形容詞を取り、SVCの文型を作る。よって、bの副詞beautifullyは形容詞beautifulであるべき。feel「感じる」、sound「聞こえる」、smell「匂いがする」とともに覚えておこう。（SVC構文に関して、問題97参照）

---

198. Concerned parties complained what this horror film should not have been
    _____   ____
            a   b
   made available to minors, even if accompanied by their parents.
   _____ _____
              c   d

答：b (what → that) このホラー映画は、たとえ親の同伴があったとしても、子供たちには公開されるべきではなかったと、懸念のぬぐえない人たちは不平を述べた。

198．接続詞 that
下線部bにあるwhatは先行詞を含む関係代名詞であるから、これは名詞句ということになる（問題67参照）。しかし、動詞complainは分類上自動詞なので、そのまま名詞句を目的語とはせず、aboutやofという前置詞を介して目的語を取るか、that節を後続させて不平の内容を示す。下線部b以下には、不平の内容を表す節があるので、whatは接続詞thatに取って代わられるべきである。また、同様の問題として、thatではなくwhatが正解になるケースもあるので注意しよう。

199. The develop of a new teaching method requires much research.
　　　　ā　　b̄　　　　　　　　　　　　　c̄　　　d̄

答：b（develop → development）新しい教授法の開発には、多くの研究が必要だ。

199.　the ＋名詞
　冠詞がつくのはふつう名詞である。この文中の develop は「発展させる、開発する」という動詞であるから、これに the がつくのはおかしい。よって、名詞形 development にするべき。

200. The high up we go, the colder it becomes.
　　　　ā　　　b̄　c̄　　　d̄

答：a（high up → higher up）高く行けば行くほど、寒くなる。

200.　the -er, the -er
　「～すればするほど、…である」というときのパターン。比較級に the がついたものが2つ並ぶ構文である。よって、high up を higher up に直せばよい。

PART 2

Notes

Note 1：Heavy NP-Shift（NP = Noun Phrase（名詞句））

　副詞的要素はふつう他動詞と直接目的語の間には入れない。よって（1a）は正しいが、（1b）はそうでない（＊は正しくない文の印）。

(1) a.　My friend told me to drink tea every night.
　　 b.　*My friend told me to drink every night tea.

（1b）が文法的でないのは、他動詞 drink とその目的語 tea の間に every night という副詞的な要素が割り込んでいるからである。しかしながら、目的語が長くなると(2)に見られるようにこれが許容されてしまう。

(2)　　My friend told me to drink every night three cups of tea with a slice of lemon.

これは(3)に示されるように、目的語の文末への移動として捕らえられ、heavy な名詞句（つまり長い名詞句）のみに見られる移動現象（Heavy NP-Shift）として説明されることがある。

(3) a.　*My friend told me to drink ＿ every night tea.
　　 b.　My friend told me to drink ＿ every night three cups of tea with a slice of lemon.

確かに目的語が長いときは、Heavy NP-Shift を適用したほうが文の座りがよくなるし、問題5に見られるように適用しないと副詞がどの動詞にかかるのかがわかりにくくなってしまうものもある。

(4)（＝問題5）
　　 a.　We should check that there are no careless mistakes before we turn in our exams carefully.
　　 b.　We should check carefully that there are no careless mistakes before we turn in our exams.

(4a) では下線を施された that 節が check のすぐ後にあり、他動詞＋目的語の語順が保たれているが、副詞 carefully が turn in にかかるという解釈も構造上可能になり、直ちに check を修飾していると読み取るのが困難になってしまう。そこで Heavy NP-Shift を使い下線の that 節を文末に移動し、(4b) の形を導く。こうすれば、carefully がかかるのは check であることが一目瞭然となるのである。
　Heavy NP-Shift は、SVOO や SVOC の文型（特に OO と OC の語順において）にも利用され

ることあるが、メカニズムはここに見たものとまったく同じ。読みやすい英文を書くのにも必要なテクニックなので、ぜひ覚えておこう。（どのくらい長ければheavyな名詞句とみなされるかに関しては、はっきりした基準がない。洗練された英文をたくさん読み、コツを肌で感じ取れるようにしたい。）

Note 2：倒置
　問題7の「肯定・否定の同意」のパターンも、結局「強調の倒置」であるとみなすことができる。これは同意を強調するため、「～もそうだ」という意味を持つso（肯定の場合）とneither（否定の場合）が文頭に来たものだと考えられるからだ。よって、それに伴う主語と助動詞の倒置というのは、問題88および89に見られる強調の倒置と何ら変わりないことになる。

Note 3：another と the other
　問題15でotherの使い方を見たが、ここではanotherとthe otherの違いを確認しておく。anotherはもともとan + otherであるから、すでに不定冠詞a(n)がついていることになる。よって、常に単数。また、the anotherということもありえない。「もう1つ」という意味を持つ語であるが、以下のような場合に使われる。

(1) 　○　○　○　…
　　　↑　↑
　　one　another

(1)が示すように、何かものが3つ以上あったとしよう。ここから1つ選ぶとき、それはoneで表される。ここで「もう1つ」選ぶ場合、どれを選ぶかに関してチョイスはいろいろある。つまり限定されていないのだ。そして、どれを選んだとしても、それがanotherになる。
　これに対して、最初から2つしかものがなかったとしよう。(2)を見てほしい。

(2) 　○　○
　　　↑　↑
　　one　the other

最初の1つはone。さて「もう1つ」となった場合、今回はチョイスが限られている。1つしか残っていないのだから、選ばれるものはすでに限定されている。よって、定冠詞を伴ったthe otherが使われる。
　これらを取り間違えると、誤ったメッセージを送ってしまうことになるので、英作文および英会話では気をつけよう。

Note 4：関係節の制限的用法・非制限的用法

以下の文を見比べよう。

(1) I met a professor <u>who teaches a linguistics course at the college</u>.
(2) I met Mike's wife, <u>who teaches a linguistics course at the college</u>.

(1)、(2)ともに下線を施された部分が関係節で、(1)のほうはカンマを伴わず、(2)のほうは伴っている。(1)では、関係節が先行詞のa professorを修飾し、たくさんいる教授の中で、「その大学で言語学を教えている教授」というように、ある特定の教授を<u>指定する役割を果たしている</u>。一方、(2)では先行詞である「マイクの奥さん」に<u>補足的説明を加えるのみ</u>。前者の用法を制限的用法、後者を非制限的用法と呼ぶ。制限的用法は、先行詞の指す人やものが聞き手に知られていない場合に使われ、非制限的用法はすでに知られているときに使われる。実際、a professorというときは、聞き手は具体的にどの教授であるかをあらかじめ知らないであろうし、Mike's wifeと言えば、マイクが誰で、また彼が既婚であることは聞き手にわかっているはずである（さもなければ、いきなりMike's wifeなどと言わないであろう）。

もし、(2)においてカンマを使わず、制限的用法を使ったらどうなるか。これは、複数いるMike's wivesの内、どの奥さんのことかを聞き手にはっきりさせるために、「大学で言語学のコースを教えている奥さん」と言ったということ。

(3) I met Mike's wife <u>who teaches a linguistics course at the college</u>.

国によってはありえる状況だが、日本やアメリカではありえないので、(2)のつもりで(3)を書いたりしないように注意しよう。

Note 5：句動詞

問題79で、関係代名詞が前置詞を伴うパターンを見たが、前置詞であればどんなものでも関係代名詞に伴って先行詞の後に移動できるわけではない。以下の例を使って説明してみよう。

(1) Ken looked at the picture.
(2) Henry made up the incident.

look atは「〜を見る」、make upは「でっちあげる」という意味で、ともに動詞＋前置詞の成句（辞書によっては、ともに句動詞）として知られている。しかし、(1)と(2)には、構文上以下のような違いがある。

(3) Ken looked [at the picture].
(4) Henry [made up] the incident.

すなわち、atは後続する名詞句とともに前置詞句を作り、upはmakeと一緒になって句動詞を作る。つまりlook atは句動詞ではないのである。では、どういう証拠があるのか。ここで

前置詞を伴う関係代名詞の例が重要になる。(5)と(6)を見ていただきたい。

(5) a. The picture which Ken looked at reminded him of his old university.
　　b. The picture at which Ken looked reminded him of his old university.
(6) a. The incident which Henry made up was not true.
　　b. *The incident up which Henry made was not true.

(5b)と(6b)からわかるように、前置詞句における前置詞は関係代名詞に伴うことができるのに対し、句動詞中の前置詞はできないのである。この結果は、(3)と(4)に見られる構造上の違いを正しく反映している。すなわち、(5a)のlookedとatは句動詞というユニットを構成しないのでatはlookedを後に残して前に移動できる。これに対し、(6a)のmade upは1つのユニットを構成しているので、upはmadeを残して移動することができないのだ。

　では、一体どうやって動詞＋前置詞句（i.e. (3)のパターン）と句動詞（i.e. (4)のパターン）を見分ければよいのか。辞書に書いてあればよいのだが、ふつうこの区別はされていない。唯一の手がかりは、句動詞が他動詞の場合、目的語の後に前置詞が移動して、動詞と前置詞とで目的語をはさむことができるか、ということである。(7)に見られるように、句動詞make upではこれが可能である。

(7) Henry made the incident up.

また、この前置詞の移動は、目的語が代名詞の場合は必ず起こらなければならない。

(8) a. Henry made it up.
　　b. *Henry made up it.

これに対し、動詞と前置詞句の組み合わせの場合、前置詞の移動は一切許されない。

(9) a. *Ken looked the picture at.
　　b. *Ken looked it at.

「分離可能」といった表示を使ってこのことを多少なりとも記述している辞書もあるので、これを見たら真の句動詞であると思ってまず間違いない。そして、句動詞であれば、前置詞が関係代名詞とともに先行詞の後の位置に移動することがないと確信を持てるのである。
　しかしながら、この記述にはもれが多く、また句動詞にも例外があって、句動詞なのに目的語を動詞と前置詞とで挟み込めないもの（e.g. go over）や、常に挟み込んだ状態でしか使われないもの（e.g. get ~ through）もあるので、やはり辞書には、このような大事な情報のすべてを明記してもらいたいものである。

Note 6：形容詞の限定的用法と叙述的用法

形容詞は、名詞の直前に置かれる場合と、述語として使われる場合がある。(1)におけるpretty が前者の例で、(2)におけるそれが後者の例である。

(1) Karen is a pretty girl.
(2) Karen is pretty.

(1)に見られるように形容詞が名詞を直接修飾するとき、その形容詞は「限定的に使われている」という。また、(2)のようにSVC構文のC（補語）の役割を果たすとき、その形容詞は「叙述的に使われている」という。そして、形容詞はふつうどちらの用法も持つのだが、中には例外があって、片方の用法しか持たないものもある。ここにいくつか例を挙げておく。限定的用法しか持たないもの：main、total、sheer。叙述的用法しか持たないもの：alike、asleep、adrift。

Note 7：need の使い方

動詞 need の主語がものである場合、目的語の位置には動名詞も to 不定詞も来ることが可能だが、to 不定詞の場合は必ず受身になる。e.g. This house needs repairing/to be repaired.「この家は修繕が必要だ。」

Note 8：concerned

この単語は、もともと過去分詞であり、問題60で見たように、形容詞的に使われることが可能。しかし、単独で名詞の後につくことができる点で他と異なっている。この場合、「関係している、当該の」という意味を持つ。e.g. the people concerned「関係者たち」

また、普通の形容詞のように名詞の前につくこともももちろん可能で、この場合は「心配そうな、気遣っている」という意味になる。e.g. the concerned parents「心配している親たち」

Note 9：文法的に単数である証拠

問題131で「every や each のついたものは単数扱いになる」ということを書いたが、複数代名詞 they で受けることが可能であるとなると、果たしてこのルールにはどんな裏づけがあるのか、という疑問が出てくる。以下の例を見てみよう。

(1) Everybody loves themselves.

確かに everybody「みんな」は、意味の上では複数なので、この例のように複数（再帰）代名詞 themselves で受けることが一般的である。しかし、動詞に注目してほしい。三単現の -s がついているのである。これは、いくら everybody が意味上複数であっても、文法上は単数なので、必ず動詞は単数の形になるということを意味する。実際 *Everybody love themselves はアウトだ。また、every が直接つく名詞も単数でなければならない。every boy はよいが、*every boys はありえない（問題12で見たようなケースは除いて）。また、もちろん(2)のよう

な文もOKである。
　(2) Everybody loves himself.

　(2)におけるhimselfは単数なので、everybodyと文法上数の一致が成立する。実際アメリカの学校文法は、(2)のほうが文法的で、(1)は（特にライティングにおいては）避けられるべきであるとしている。
　しかし、問題はhimselfの性である。everybodyと言った場合、男も女も含むのに、男性のみを表すhimselfを使うのはおかしい、という議論が出てくるからだ。そこで、苦肉の策として、himself/herself、him/herself、また、Everybody thinks (s)he is smartなどという工夫がされるようになったが、これもあまりすっきりしていないので、避けられるべきだと言い出す文章家も現れ、事態は混沌としている。このことからも、代名詞に関する限り、性がニュートラルであるtheyが一般に広く受け入れられているのは、everybodyの意味が複数であるという理由に加えて、当然なのかもしれない。

Note 10：either/neither
　これらの単語は、単独では単数なので、主語になった場合は、動詞は単数を受けることになる。e.g. If either of you sings, … ; Neither of my friends has arrived …

Note 11：boringとbored
　分詞の形容詞的用法は、日本語訳から判断してしまうと間違いを犯すことがあるので注意したい。たとえば「僕は退屈している」と言いたいとき、「〜している」という訳を間に受けて、(1)のような文を作らないこと。

　(1) I am boring.

boreは「退屈させる」という他動詞だからboringという分詞は能動的な意味の形容詞として働くので、(1)は「僕は（人を）退屈させる＝つまらない奴」という意味になる。もし、自分が退屈しているのなら、他動詞boreの理屈からいって「僕は退屈させられている」、すなわち受身の形を持つ(2)の文を導かねばならない。

　(2) I am bored.

これは、interestingとinterestedにも当てはまる論理である。つまり動詞interestは、「興味を持たせる」という他動詞なので、能動的なinterestingは「（人に）興味を持たせる＝おもしろい」、そして受動的なinterestedは「興味を持たされた＝興味がある」ということになるのである。くれぐれも「君は退屈してるみたいだね」のつもりでYou look boringなどと言わないように。侮辱と取られても仕方のない言い方だから。

Lists

(以下のリストは、代表的な語をまとめたものであって、各項目に当てはまるすべての語を網羅したものではない。)

List 1：単複同形の名詞
deer	鹿	fish	魚	sheep	羊
series	シリーズ	species	(分類上の)種		

List 2：発音で気をつけるもの

① a ではなく an を伴うもの

hour	時間	heir	相続人	herbal	薬草の
honor	名誉				

② an ではなく a を伴うもの

eucalyptus	ユーカリ（の木）	eulogy	賛辞
euphemistic	婉曲的な	European	欧州の
unicorn	一角獣	uniform	制服
university	大学	universal	全世界の
union	結合、組合		

List 3：要求・命令の形容詞

advisable	賢明な	advised	勧められる
best	最もよい	crucial	必須の
desirable	望ましい	essential	不可欠の
imperative	成されねばならない	important	重要な
mandatory	義務的な	necessary	必要な
obligatory	義務的な	proposed	提案される
recommended	推奨される	required	要求される
suggested	提案される	urgent	急を要する
vital	肝要な		

List 4：要求・命令の動詞

advise	忠告する	ask	頼む
command	命令する	decree	（法令で）命ずる
demand	要求する	desire	強く望む
insist	要求する	move	提案する
order	命令する	prefer	～であることを好む
propose	提案する	recommend	推奨する
request	リクエストする	require	必要とする
stipulate	要求する	suggest	提案する
urge	～するよう強く迫る		

List 5：to不定詞を取る動詞

afford	～する余裕がある	agree	～するのに同意する
appear	～のように見える	care	～したいと思う
claim	～であると主張する	decide	～する決心をする
demand	～する／あるように要求する	deserve	～するに値する
desire	～することを強く望む	expect	～するつもりである
fail	～し損なう	happen	たまたま～する
hesitate	～するのに躊躇する	hope	～するのを希望する
learn	～できるようになる	manage	～を何とかやり遂げる
offer	～しようと申し出る	plan	～するつもりである
prepare	～する準備をする	pretend	～するふりをする
refuse	～することを拒む	seem	～するように思われる
strive	～しようと努力する	tend	～する傾向がある
threaten	～すると言って脅す	volunteer	～しようと進んで申し出る
wait	～するのを待つ	want	～したい
wish	～することを望む		

List 6：to不定詞、動名詞ともに取る動詞

① to不定詞と動名詞とで意味の変わらないもの

⁺attempt	試みる	begin	始める
(can't) bear	耐える（られない）	(can't) stand	耐える（られない）
continue	続ける	dread	恐れる
hate	嫌う	⁺intend	つもりである
like	好きである	love	大好きである
⁺neglect	怠る	prefer	好む
start	始める		

（⁺これらの動詞は、to不定詞を取ることのほうが多い。）

② to不定詞と動名詞とで意味の変わるもの

	to不定詞	動名詞
forget	～するのを忘れる	～したのを忘れる
mean	～するつもりである	～することを意味する
quit (stop)	～するためにしていることを止める	～することを止める
regret	～するのを残念に思う	～したことを後悔する
remember	～するのを忘れないでおく	～したことを覚えている
try	～しようとする	～してみる

List 7：動名詞のみを取る動詞

admit	認める	anticipate	予期する
appreciate	ありがたく思う	avoid	避ける
cannot help	～せずにはいられない	complete	仕上げる
consider	熟慮する	defer	延期する
delay	遅らせる	deny	否定する
detest	ひどく嫌う	discuss	話し合う
dislike	嫌う	enjoy	楽しむ
escape	のがれる	excuse	許す
finish	終える	forgive	許す
imagine	想像する	involve	必然的に含む
keep (on)	～し続ける	mention	述べる
mind	気にする	miss	～できないのを寂しく思う
postpone	延期する	practice	実行する、練習する
recall	思い出す	report	報告する
resent	憤慨する	resist	抵抗する
resume	再び始める	suggest	提案する
tolerate	許容する		

List 8：慣例的に the のつくもの

① 複数形の国、島、湖、山など
- the Alps　　　　　　アルプス山脈　　　the Great Lakes　　五大湖
- the Hawaiian Islands　ハワイ諸島　　　the Philippines　　フィリピン

② 海、川、砂漠など
- the Gobi Desert　　　ゴビ砂漠　　　　the Pacific Ocean　太平洋
- the Persian Gulf　　　ペルシャ湾　　　the Potomac River　ポトマック川
- the Suez Canal　　　スエズ運河

③ 博物館、図書館、橋など
- the British Museum　大英博物館　　　the Golden Gate Bridge　金門橋
- the Louvre　　　　　ルーブル美術館

④ 大学名など（of を伴うもの）
- the Department of Agriculture　農学科　　the School of Education　教育学部
- the University of Texas　　テキサス大学

⑤ 戦争
- the Korean War　　　朝鮮戦争　　　　the Russo-Japanese War　日露戦争
- the Vietnam War　　ベトナム戦争

⑥ 人種
- the Chinese　　　　中国人　　　　　the Germans　　　ドイツ人
- the Japanese　　　日本人

PART 3

Practice Test 1

Directions: Questions 1-15 are incomplete sentences. Beneath each sentence, you will see four words or phrases, marked a, b, c, and d. Choose the **one** word or phrase that best completes the sentence.

1. ------- studied the art of healing with bones dug from caves.

    a. Mary with whom John
    b. That is Mary with whom
    c. We know Mary who did
    d. It is Mary who

2. Marge had a ------- with a garden.

    a. condominium expensive
    b. cute apartment
    c. house beautifully
    d. to live in a cave attaching to

3. Roger won't be going to the concert, and ------- .

    a. his friends will too
    b. so do his friends
    c. his friends did, either
    d. neither will his friends

4. If ------- at all, I would not have failed all the subjects as I did this year.

    a. had I studied
    b. I studied
    c. I were to study
    d. I had studied

5. Dr. May had a hunch that puberty was starting much earlier ------- .

    a. as we thought it to be
    b. than the textbooks said
    c. so as to revising his theory
    d. with his teachers had taught him

6. Karen has kept ------- own video diary, in which she documents her challenges and emotions.

    a. she
    b. her
    c. hers
    d. the

7. This university, ------- , has more than 100,000 students.

    a. the largest of all the schools in the Tokyo area
    b. is the biggest in Osaka
    c. which the student body is the most numerous
    d. it is not for everybody

8. NASA's long-range plans call for sampling hidden pools of Martian water ------- .

    a. provided with NASA is given certain information
    b. if they exist at all
    c. concerning its new rocket project is successful
    d. the condition under which NASA works

9. Nick called the police after ------- pictures of an armed man at the photo store where he worked.

    a. the notification
    b. he has noticed
    c. noticing
    d. which it is noticed

10. That half-hour TV series ------- , but it is usually shown on a weekday night at 11.

    a. has moved over the years
    b. are sometimes broadcast on weekends
    c. have been very popular with early birds
    d. are planned to be canceled soon

11. Earlier Saturday, the Navy ------- the sunken ship, using an underwater vehicle.

    a. has declared that it has found
    b. announced that it had located
    c. is scheduled to have a press conference about
    d. will issue an official statement regarding

12. The director knows that for a movie to be full of life, it must above all concern ------- with specific lives.

    a. himself
    b. its life
    c. itself
    d. it

13. What is surprising about this renovation is that the language lab has been ------- updated.

    a. technologically
    b. computational
    c. a very expensive
    d. really remarkable

14. If the professor ------- afternoon classes, he holds office hours in the morning.

    a. will teach
    b. would prefer
    c. has
    d. will be scheduled to offer

15. The salary of my mother is ------- .

    a. as much as my teacher
    b. higher than that of my father
    c. less than me
    d. much fewer than a university professor

Directions: In questions 16-40 each sentence has four underlined words or phrases. The four underlined parts of the sentence are marked a, b, c, and d. Identify the **one** underlined word or phrase that must be changed in order for the sentence to be correct.

16. According to one survey, American teenagers are far <u>most likely</u> than
                                                                                   a
    their European peers <u>to use marijuana and other illicit drugs</u>, but
                                                        b
    European teenagers are <u>more likely</u> to smoke cigarettes and
                                             c
    <u>drink alcohol</u>.
        d

17. <u>Almost every</u> cell of your body <u>contain</u> coiled-up DNA—the
         a   b
    <u>famous twisting</u> ladder of genetic instructions that <u>is</u> three billion
          c   d
    rungs long.

18. Although <u>many kinds</u> of <u>musical instruments</u> are used by rock
                 a   b
    musicians, <u>the</u> electric guitar seems to be the most popular among
                c
    <u>itself</u>.
     d

19. Childhood <u>play</u> is about learning and discovery, and batteries are not
             a
    always required for <u>child</u> to put <u>imagination</u> to <u>work</u>.
                  b   c   d

20. Criminal <u>gangs operating</u> in Turkey and Iraq <u>seem to have been</u>
             a   b
    behind <u>to smuggle</u> many kinds of illegal drugs <u>into France</u>.
           c   d

21. <u>Each</u> of the immigrant mothers encountered <u>different sort</u> of <u>trouble</u>
      a   b   c
    in trying to bring up her own <u>offspring</u> on American soil.
                                 d

22. He talked about it the fact that someone has been dumping
        _____   a   _____
                                                         b
thousands of tons of water from the city's reservoirs.
_____   _____
            c   d

23. If you want to know whether passengers would be willing to pay
                                              _____
                                                  a
$200 more to avoid flight delays, asking them; they will certainly say no.
_____   _____   _____
      b   c   d

24. In one of those twists of fate that only seems to happen in fiction,
                                                 _____ _____
                                                      a   b
Miss White actually fell in love with one of her own students.
_____   _____
         c   d

25. Miss White is very proud of John and Mary, because both student are
                     _____   _____
                           a   b
actively involved in her "Don't Drink and Drive" project.
_____   ___
        c   d

26. Mr. Tanaka has decided to write to manager to complain about the
                 _____   _____
                       a   b
very rude behavior of several waiters at a restaurant in Chicago's
                                      _____   _____
                                              c   d
O'Hare Airport.

27. One day after the big earthquake hit Santa Ana, El Salvador, two
                                         ___
                                          a
rescue teams from Chile arrived there, and team from Spain
                                           ____
                                             b
were expected the following day.
_____ _____
      c   d

28. The University of Michigan's "Monitoring the Future" project is
        _____
                                     a
considered the most relying barometer of student drug-use trends.
_____   _____ _____   _____
    b   c   d

29. The airlines are only going to send planes to places where they think
    ‾‾‾‾‾‾‾‾   ‾‾‾‾‾‾‾‾‾‾‾
         a   b
   there are going to be passengers, and passengers will only go
                                                  ‾‾‾‾‾‾‾‾‾
                                                      c
   where are planes.
   ‾‾‾‾‾‾‾‾‾‾‾‾‾‾‾
           d

30. The author's intention is to present us with a stereotyped character
                          ‾‾‾‾‾   ‾‾‾‾‾‾‾‾‾‾‾
                            a   b
   and then slowly reveal to we our own misconceptions.
                         ‾‾‾‾‾‾ ‾‾‾‾‾‾‾‾‾‾‾‾‾‾‾‾‾‾‾
                           c   d

31. The developed nations of the world have already enjoyed the most
    ‾‾‾‾‾‾‾‾‾‾‾‾‾‾‾‾‾‾‾‾‾   ‾‾‾‾‾‾‾
              a   b
   dramatic improvement in life expectancy in the human history.
                           ‾‾‾‾‾‾‾‾‾‾‾‾‾‾‾   ‾‾‾‾‾‾‾‾‾‾‾‾‾‾‾‾
                                  c   d

32. The religious cult's teachings are viewed critically by other cult
                        ‾‾‾‾‾‾‾‾‾   ‾‾‾‾‾‾‾‾‾‾
                            a   b
   despite the fact that the cult in question now claims to have as many
   ‾‾‾‾‾‾‾‾‾‾‾‾‾‾‾‾‾‾‾‾‾   ‾‾‾‾‾‾‾‾‾‾‾‾
               c   d
   as 10,000 followers.

33. The rise in global temperatures in recent decades has already had
                                    ‾‾‾‾‾‾‾‾‾‾‾‾‾‾‾‾ ‾‾‾
                                            a   b
   impact on wildlife, glaciers, sea ice and other features of the earth.
   ‾‾‾‾‾‾   ‾‾‾‾‾‾‾‾‾‾‾‾‾‾‾‾‾‾‾‾‾‾‾‾‾‾‾‾‾
      c   d

34. The second song collection is slight more abstract than the first,
               ‾‾‾‾‾‾‾‾‾‾‾‾‾‾‾   ‾‾‾‾‾‾
                      a   b
   not insisting as strongly on making the complex implications of
   ‾‾‾‾‾‾‾‾‾‾‾‾‾
         c
   Japanese rhythm fit into that of Indonesia.
                  ‾‾‾
                   d

35. The writer announced rather grand that his recent novel
                              ―――― ―――
                                a   b
    is based upon the life of William Wallace, a Scottish national hero.
    ――――――――   ――――――――――――――――――――――――――――
        c   d

36. This movie, which appears to be about a lawsuit, it is not really about
                                                     ―― ―――――――
                                                      a   b
    a lawsuit but about a person who cannot seem to reconcile how she
                                     ―――――――――――――――――――――
                                                  c
    views herself with how others view her.
                                  ―――――――
                                     d

37. Various technology such as the global positioning satellite system have
            ――――――――――   ―――――――――――――――――――
                 a   b
    been developed to make flying and air traffic control more efficient.
                    ―――――――――――   ―――――――――――――
                         c   d

38. Water remains liquid in Lake Rhye because the thick ice blanket on
              ――――――――――――   ―――――――――
                   a   b
    its surface insulates it against the 60-degree below zero air
    temperate of the polar region and traps heat that flows up from the Earth.
    ――――――――――   ――――――――――
         c   d

39. The wine business is booming, and it is no wonder that despite
                      ――――――――――
                          a
    some highly fees, all the wine classes at cooking schools around the
    ――――――――――――   ――――――――――――
          b   c
    nation are packed.
           ――――――――――
               d

40. As expected, press reactions to the horror movie were
                                 ――――――――――――――――――――
                                           a
    as wildly varied as the public who flocked to see it.
    ―――――――――――――   ――――――――――   ―――――――
          b   c   d

Practice Test 2

Directions: Questions 1-15 are incomplete sentences. Beneath each sentence, you will see four words or phrases, marked a, b, c, and d. Choose the **one** word or phrase that best completes the sentence.

1. Another way delays could ------- would be by flying fewer planes.

    a. cut
    b. be cut
    c. be cutting
    d. have been cutting

2. Catherine Ball, ------- , has been convicted of fraud and perjury.

    a. an herbal supplement marketer
    b. an European drug dealer
    c. an union representative
    d. a heir to his lover's fortune

3. An expert in bacteriology, ------- to investigate the cause of yellow fever.

    a. it was reported that Dr. Mitchell was to arrive in Ghana
    b. everybody believed that Dr. Flexner would visit Ghana
    c. those doctors left for Ghana
    d. Dr. Noguchi went to Ghana

4. Poor Takashi ------- on what was supposed to be their first date.

    a. would be punched and Mary kicked him too
    b. punched in the face and kick Mary also
    c. was punched and kicked by Mary
    d. may be punched but Mary will surely kick

5. Michael ------- .

    a. has a lot of money, handsome, and everybody likes him
    b. is rich, handsome, and popular
    c. seems to be a millionaire, works as a model, and very popular
    d. appears to earn a lot, has many lovers, and he is liked by many

6. We should all learn to speak English and ------- clearly in the language.

   a. to express ourselves
   b. voicing our opinions
   c. our thoughts be conveyed
   d. it must be spoken

7. We would like to hire American workers unless there is a compelling reason ------- .

   a. for hiring them no way
   b. of no foreigner necessarily
   c. with never accepting them
   d. not to

8. ------- , the researcher approached the big tiger in the cage.

   a. Cautiously but a smooth manner
   b. With a lot of careful but tenderly
   c. In gradualness but unhurriedly
   d. Slowly and carefully

9. That lazy professor read ------- most of his students did last year.

   a. half only textbooks
   b. only half as many books as
   c. no fewer academic papers rather than
   d. less than ten reference books comparing

10. The recent expansion of Mr. Flexner's business to Southeast Asia brought ------- more fame and fortune.

   a. it
   b. itself
   c. him
   d. down

11. Roger is not happy that he has to write two term papers this semester, but Brian has to write ------- , and he thinks nothing of it.

    a. twice as many
    b. twice that much
    c. two times much more
    d. as two times more as

12. The first long-term study of the asteroid, ------- , was a relatively cheap mission.

    a. which costing $223 million
    b. which costed $223 million
    c. $223 million cost
    d. costing $223 million

13. Mr. Fargo expects this court to convene on or about ------- in Pearl Harbor, Hawaii.

    a. 22 of Thursday February
    b. Thursday the 22nd of February
    c. the 22nd of the February Thursday
    d. the 22nd Thursday of February

14. Some experts hope the new experiment will lead to powerful new genetic medicines ------- a huge variety of illnesses and conditions.

    a. to tackle
    b. for tackling with
    c. for the purpose of tackle
    d. to some extent of tackling

15. Mr. Deacon is a lawyer, a politician, ------- .

    a. with his wife being a teacher
    b. but works as a teacher as well
    c. but teaches very well
    d. and a teacher

Directions: In questions 16-40 each sentence has four underlined words or phrases. The four underlined parts of the sentence are marked a, b, c, and d. Identify the **one** underlined word or phrase that must be changed in order for the sentence to be correct.

16. According to the journalist, a single corporate layoff of a few thousands workers, likely to be spread over a period of a few weeks
                                              a   b
    to many months, has a minimal effect on the economy of the nation.
                        c   d

17. After reading Mr. Clark's story, where was called "She must be out of
         a   b   c
    her mind!," the children asked for more stories.
                              d

18. Asked by the court if he would have swear to tell the truth, Mr.
              a   b   c
    Taylor replied, "I affirm all my answers will be true."
                                  d

19. Believing that Santa Claus does exist, it is thought the children are
                              a   b
    behaving themselves in order to receive what they want
               c
    for Christmas.
       d

20. Dorothy is a first-rate student; she takes biology advance, plays
              a   b
    electric guitar and wants to go to college.
          c   d

21. It was a very touching moment which the graduating students all
                              a
    expressed appreciation for the professional and moral contribution
           b
    that their professors had made to them.
     c   d

22. Kathy claims to be still mourning the recent death of her husband,
    ───────
       a
    that makes it odd that she held such a lavish and jolly party the other
    ────   ──────────   ────
     b   c   d
    day.

23. Locating in Tokyo and nicknamed "Paradise," the university accepts
    ────────
       a
    virtually all applicants who wish to enroll there.
    ────────────   ─── ──────────────
         b   c   d

24. Mr. Schindler left Vienna in 1914 to work in Chicago, which he was
                   ───────────   ─────
                        a   b
    heavily influenced by Frank Lloyd Wright.
    ────────────────── ──
            c   d

25. Mrs. Jarvis, principal of Bill Clinton High School, reports significant
                ──────────────────────────────────────
                                    a
    results from its school's Adopt-a-Senior Program.
            ──── ───   ──────────────────────
             b   c   d

26. Residents of the city have complained since years that the red
                         ─────────────── ─────
                                a   b
    double-decker buses clog neighborhood streets with fumes and
                                                      ─────
                                                        c
    tourists gawking into apartment windows.
            ───────
               d

27. Some of the details of the author's life have been weave into this book,
                                              ──────── ─────
                                                 a   b
    like the discovery that her mother had left behind two other daughters
    ────   ──────────────────────────
     c   d
    when she came to the United States from Kagoshima in 1949.

28. The airline industry was quick to respond to the criticism, said that
                                                  a   b
    new technology would have to be implemented before customers
                             c
    saw a significant change.
           d

29. The lack of human dignity experiencing by Africans is the direct
                a   b
    result of the policy of white supremacy.
           c   d

30. The spacecraft was launched into space on top of a rocket in 1996 and
                        a   b   c
    has traveled 2 billion miles before then.
                          d

31. The students had expected to hear very excited tales from the speaker,
                    a   b
    who instead told them a very boring story about life insurance.
                          c   d

32. The two robbers disappeared after they were interviewed from
                              a   b
    investigators on Thursday and agreed to have their fingerprints taken.
           c   d

33. There is no scientific evidence in that shows that playing Mozart to a
                                a   b   c
    baby at the age of one is going to change its brain cells.
                                    d

34. This airline has been excellent in providing available the lowest fares
                              a   b
    when booking and in responding to customer complaints within 60
           c   d
    days.

35. This is an album of which a 19th-century style Vietnamese music that
                     ───────
                        a
    emerged when what is now Ho Chi Minh City swelled with migrants
                 ──────────────────────────── ──────────── ────────
                               b   c   d
    from northern Vietnam and China.

36. This news story is about a high school where students turned in three
                                            ─────   ─────────
                                              a   b
    of their classmates who had been bragging about their plans of attack
                             ────────────────   ──────────────
                                     c   d
    their school.

37. This novel is about a Chinese-American woman who 10-year
                                                 ─── ───────
                                                  a   b
    relationship with the man she loves is deteriorating for reasons she
                                        ──   ───
                                         c   d
    doesn't understand.

38. This report is the second in a series of three voluminous documents
                                               ────────────────────────
                                                         a
    that provide first thorough assessment of climate data in ten years.
                 ───── ────────   ────────────
                   b   c   d

39. We are having trouble finding a push toy for toddlers, the kind for
               ──────────────   ───
                    a   b
    toddlers push along when they are learning to walk.
                 ─────   ────────
                   c   d

40. We expect a general rebound in PC sales in the second half of the
                  ────────────── ───────────
                        a   b
    year, which Microsoft releases its new operating system and Intel
          ──────────────────────────
                       c
    distributes its new Pentium 4 chip more widely.
    ──────────
        d

Practice Test 3

Directions: Questions 1-15 are incomplete sentences. Beneath each sentence, you will see four words or phrases, marked a, b, c, and d. Choose the **one** word or phrase that best completes the sentence.

1. This book contains six practice tests; take them under testing conditions, exactly as you ------- on the day of the actual test next month.

    a. had
    b. have
    c. did
    d. will

2. The President has insisted ------- any money she received as bribes.

    a. on his brother's return
    b. to return for his lover's
    c. that his sister return
    d. if he is to return

3. Some of Mr. Bond's children were ------- all day, and Mr. Bond was upset.

    a. acting up
    b. acting up to
    c. making up to
    d. making up with

4. Mr. Clinton's relationship with that actress appears ------- .

    a. back well with the year 1980
    b. to go back well before 1980
    c. ended before he became President of the United States
    d. well before the presidential election to be over

5. According to Mr. Mercury, fate and individual choice ------- .

    a. separated from utterly things
    b. absolutely things of separation
    c. are entirely separate things
    d. will certainly different matters

6. Jane's knowledge of international relations makes ------- .

   a. interesting to numerous agencies her
   b. it charming for most men her talent
   c. her attractive to many companies
   d. it worthwhile her marketability

7. This is the house where ------- lived together.

   a. along with the Taylors, accompanied by Brian and John,
   b. the Taylors as well as two of their friends, Brian and John,
   c. for Brian and John, coupled with the Taylors of Briton,
   d. with Brian and John, the Taylors as well,

8. Mr. Gittes, a private detective, was trying very hard to ------- .

   a. keep from his client being molested
   b. save his client for getting to murder him
   c. keep his client from being arrested
   d. save his time meeting his client's absurdly demand

9. Everybody knows that the late president of the company ------- a man of his word.

   a. has been
   b. is
   c. was
   d. will be

10. One way to cut flight delays would be to fly fewer planes, and this might ------- to all airlines.

   a. seem practical
   b. help conveniently
   c. reduce costly
   d. improve efficiently

11. The coroner's report proves that the murder victim ------- in his lungs when he was killed.

    a. containing contaminated water
    b. with too much alcohol
    c. who somehow managed to drain rain water
    d. had salt water

12. Only by hard work ------- .

    a. will he be able to accomplish that task
    b. he managed to buy a house
    c. finally she succeeded in getting her professor's attention
    d. solved she this very difficult math problem

13. We associate Tokyo ------- crowded with people and countless small buildings.

    a. with small places
    b. along a busy city
    c. as the tiny capital
    d. similar to New York

14. Since they are full-time students, we tend to expect them to study hard every day, but in reality, they ------- .

    a. no study at all
    b. sure skip classes
    c. absolute are lazy people
    d. rarely do

15. My girlfriend, along with her parents and her brother, ------- America on the 23rd of March.

    a. have returned from
    b. are to visit
    c. is scheduled to leave for
    d. have already arrived in

Directions: In questions 16-40 each sentence has four underlined words or phrases. The four underlined parts of the sentence are marked a, b, c, and d. Identify the **one** underlined word or phrase that must be changed in order for the sentence to be correct.

16. The number of individual donors pledged to give $1 million or more
         a   b   c
    to the university library in 2000, according to data reported by *the*
                                                        d
    Japan Times.

17. According to the scientist, even if the most commoner causes of death
                                                    a   b
    —cancer, heart disease and stroke—were eliminated, the increase in
    life expectancy would be no more than 15 years.
          c   d

18. As like most academic institutions, this university
       a
    requires its students to write a graduation thesis by the end of their
              b   c   d
    eighth semester.

19. By the time the rock guitarist died of prostate cancer at the year of 66
         a   b   c
    in 1983, his reputation had ebbed.
                               d

20. If the council and mayor choose their superintendent wisely, they
                                          a
    should be able to handle matters school without
          b   c
    too much of a problem.
          d

21. In response to written questions from the police this week,
    $\underset{a}{\overline{}}$
    an attorney for Carson Dyle indicated she had given
    $\underset{b}{\overline{}}\underset{c}{\overline{}}$
    sum of enormous money to Mr. Keeton's library.
    $\underset{d}{\overline{}}$

22. It was mandatory at that university that all Ph.D. students

    would write at least two papers of a publishable quality before
    $\underset{a}{\overline{}}\underset{b}{\overline{}}$
    advancing to the status of ABD.
    $\underset{c}{\overline{}}\underset{d}{\overline{}}$

23. It was possible for the company in Tokyo to begin on using the
    $\underset{a}{\overline{}}$
    abbreviated name of S.O.S. because no other major corporations in
    $\underset{b}{\overline{}}\underset{c}{\overline{}}$
    Japan had laid claim to it.
    $\underset{d}{\overline{}}$

24. Mr. Lucather is a tireless advocate of a performance-based pay scale
    $\underset{a}{\overline{}}$
    and has probably done more to replace his company's age-based pay
    $\underset{b}{\overline{}}$
    scale with it than any other individuals.
    $\underset{c}{\overline{}}\underset{d}{\overline{}}$

25. Mr. Rogers made the same prediction like mine about the future of
    $\underset{a}{\overline{}}\underset{b}{\overline{}}\underset{c}{\overline{}}$
    the children at the kindergarten, for a slightly different reason.
    $\underset{d}{\overline{}}$

26. My father's idea of the most best education a young man could get
    $\underset{a}{\overline{}}\underset{b}{\overline{}}\underset{c}{\overline{}}$
    was Princeton and Yale, for some reason.
    $\underset{d}{\overline{}}$

27. Not only the younger actresses resembled their older counterparts
    ———————————a—————————— ———————b———————
    in looks and screen behavior, but there were also real off-screen
    ———c———   ——————d——————
    similarities between them.

28. Mr. Page has been friends with Mr. Bush since high school, but he
            ———a——— ———b———   ————c————
    says he still calls his old friend as "Mr. President."
                       ————d————

29. One by one, historic signs were chosen to restored be and
                                ——————a—————— ——————b——————
    brought back to their old glory by the new neon company.
    ——————————c——————————   ————————d————————

30. Professor Gold lit his cigarette in the classroom, even it was
                   —a—   ————b————
    prohibited and it would certainly annoy some of his students.
                    ————c———— ————d————

31. Scientists are now particularly interested in the results of a survey on
                ——————————a—————————   —b—
    marijuana use in the Netherlands, which is a country known to its
    ——————c——————   ——d——
    relatively permissive drug laws.

32. Sky Plaza, an intimate bar with authentic glitter and live music, is
                                ————————————a———————————————
    there I fell in love with a girl for the first time in my life.
    ——b—— ———c———   ———————————d——————————

33. The diplomat spends a great number of time in Geneva, where he has
                        ——————a—————   ——————b——————
    numerous opportunities to meet with foreign dignitaries.
    ———c————   ——————d——————

34. The writer says she has done the research yet for her next novel, and
                                                  a   b
    expects to begin writing it in two weeks.
                  c   d

35. Those students were looking forward to take advantage of their new
                                              a
    teacher's relative ignorance of how to handle students of their age.
            b   c   d

36. When casinos, motels, restaurants and businesses wanted new signs,
       a   b
    the old ones were aside cast.
        c   d

37. When the politicians were interviewed on TV, they
                                  a
    positioned themselves as near to the cameras that they could get.
           b   c   d

38. Within the meteorite was a mix of helium and argon gases similar to
            a   b
    that found in certain stars but not alike anything that could form
      c   d
    naturally on Earth.

39. Yoshio was very surprised to find out that his English teacher's
            a   b
    TOEFL scores were exactly the same of his own.
                   c   d

40. Your composition, which is full of grammatical and spelling errors,
                                      a
    certainly needs of rewriting before it can be resubmitted.
        b   c   d

Practice Test 4

Directions: Questions 1-15 are incomplete sentences. Beneath each sentence, you will see four words or phrases, marked a, b, c, and d. Choose the **one** word or phrase that best completes the sentence.

1. Members of the admissions office differed ------- which applicants to accept.

    a. from
    b. with
    c. over
    d. than

2. That home-delivery company's catchphrase is "It's ------- , or it's on us."

    a. without time
    b. on time
    c. timely manner
    d. one time after others

3. The President's murder was motivated by both ------- factors.

    a. money as well as jealousy
    b. envious, financial, and corporate
    c. personal and political
    d. military and economic reasons as well

4. For the upcoming picnic, we will need ------- food.

    a. only a little
    b. very few
    c. a numerous amount of
    d. a great number of

5. Mr. Fox's favorite cruises last 6 to 13 days, and fares range from $700 ------- $1,100 per person.

    a. up
    b. upward
    c. under
    d. to

6. The new bill, if passed, will greatly benefit ------- in the Tokyo area.

   a. those who own land
   b. us from the people
   c. from becoming rich by possessing land
   d. every landlord with whom

7. ------- that prestigious university passes the bar examination before graduation.

   a. All the students from
   b. Twice as many students as last year in
   c. Three of every ten students who graduate from
   d. One in four students at

8. Sometimes the two colleagues refused to ------- and communicated through notes.

   a. see theirselves
   b. talk to one other
   c. say hello to one after another
   d. speak to each other

9. There is still no sign that ------- any of the detective's questions.

   a. either of the suspects has answered
   b. neither of the culprits have even cared about
   c. either the mastermind or his accomplice are willing to hear
   d. neither the offender or the victim is going to be interrogated with

10. Karen finally realized that she had never ------- Dr. Cook's lectures in the way he wanted her to.

    a. heard about
    b. attended on
    c. enjoyed with
    d. listened to

11. In this novel, ------- the main character through the eyes of her 13-year-old son.

   a. we first encounter
   b. the reader has the firstly encounter with
   c. firstly of all, it is with
   d. it is revealed, firstly and foremost, that

12. Before the final examination, students gathered in corners, ------- .

   a. and blamed each and the other for not studying
   b. but anybody did not open their mouth
   c. whispering to one another
   d. which means one other wasn't ready to actually take it

13. Both ------- will have concerts in Taiwan.

   a. the Eagles, the Doobie Brothers, and Grand Funk
   b. the Eagles and the Doobie Brothers, Grand Funk
   c. the Eagles, the Doobie Brothers, Grand Funk as well
   d. the Eagles and the Doobie Brothers, as well as Grand Funk,

14. Freddie's jokes last week were hilarious, but the ones he told last night were ------- .

   a. even more funnier
   b. much hilariouser than that
   c. less funny
   d. lesser hilarious than before

15. In our weekly meetings, everybody argues for the sake of arguing, ------- where the discussion is going.

   a. with no idea at all
   b. which signifies assumption
   c. doesn't know
   d. to get no satisfaction from

Directions: In questions 16-40 each sentence has four underlined words or phrases. The four underlined parts of the sentence are marked a, b, c, and d. Identify the **one** underlined word or phrase that must be changed in order for the sentence to be correct.

16. A further rise in the temperature of 2.7 to 10 Fahrenheit degree could
          a   b   c
    disrupt water supplies, flood coasts, destroy coral reefs and push
    vulnerable species like the Bengal tiger to extinction.
                                               d

17. After a stormy marriage, Kevin and Winnie were divorced but,
                                                   a
    for some reason, continued on live under the same roof.
           b   c   d

18. Charged with a list of juvenile crimes, the high school dropouts were
                      a
    sentenced to between 9 to 18 months at a reform school in Los
        b   c   d
    Angeles.

19. His life has been so marked by quirks of fate that Dr. Nakamura has
                      a   b
    gradually come to believe that there are things in world that cannot
         c   d
    be explained rationally.

20. If you want to become a language teacher, you should know to speak
                                                 a
    a foreign language yourself, because then you know what it takes to
                                                   b
    acquire another language, which will surely help you when you teach.
                          c   d

21. In Janice's mysterious room, the electric heater inexplicably shuts

itself off, the television set turns on beside itself, and noises sound
      a   b   c
unexpectedly from odd places.
                  d

22. In order to improve our school's reputation, we would like to hire

able professors, but if salaries are low, we are unlikely to get
      a   b   c
well faculty members.
        d

23. In spite the growing outcry from customers, the telephone company
      a   b
is not planning to do anything about its incompetent operators.
                    c   d

24. It is necessary to split the list of universities into two to avoid
                                                                       a
to compare apples and oranges; multi-disciplinary universities have
  b
a broad focus, while science and technology schools are
                      c
more specialized.
    d

25. It is out the experience of being caught between countries and
        a   b
cultures that singers such as Gloria Estefan have begun to create
                                                  c
what is, in effect, a new genre of American music.
                    d

26. John's company has already notified <u>most of the 3,000 people</u> who
                                                                                 a
    will lose their jobs <u>as</u> part of a <u>cost-cutting</u> campaign, and Mary's
                     b   c
    plans <u>of</u> cut 1,700 jobs by the end of May.
          d

27. Many toys now <u>come with</u> <u>so much sound</u> and action that it is
                              a   b
    <u>as if we do not trust</u> children to use <u>own imagination</u>.
             c   d

28. Mr. Adams, a private English tutor, charged the president of the
    automobile company <u>on</u> <u>an</u> hourly <u>base</u>, receiving a total of about
                             a b   c
    $4,000 <u>in a week</u>.
           d

29. Mr. Dean is wondering <u>whether or not</u> his <u>three-year</u> research
                                   a   b
    experience in Tonga as a marine biologist will <u>be interested in</u> the
                                                                        c
    research institute where he wants to <u>find employment</u>.
                                                        d

30. <u>Much of what</u> might <u>be concerned with</u> some people <u>about</u> this
          a   b   c
    horror movie is not on the screen; it is in the mind and the
    imagination of <u>the viewer</u>.
                      d

31. On any <u>given to</u> <u>day</u>, there are still many <u>people visiting</u> Arlington
             a   b   c
    Cemetery, mourning the death of the <u>late</u> President Kennedy.
                                                      d

32. Pink Floyd, one of the <u>most acclaimed rock band</u> <u>of</u> the 70's, has lost
                                                 a   b
    several members <u>over</u> the years, but it <u>has not broken up officially</u>.
                        c   d

33. Scientists anticipate that <u>many people in this country today</u> <u>will live</u>
                                                             a   b
    <u>enough long</u> to witness <u>a life expectancy</u> of 85 years.
        c   d

34. Since Mr. Simmons is <u>perpetually busy</u> <u>with school chores</u>, he always
                                       a   b
    has his assistant <u>to answer</u> questions <u>from his students</u>.
                          c   d

35. Some of those very diligent students finally <u>managed to persuade</u>
                                                                a
    their English teacher <u>that</u> at least try <u>conducting</u> <u>his class all</u> in
                          b   c   d
    English.

36. Some schools in America are <u>considering lengthening</u> the school
                                              a
    <u>day or year</u> in order to <u>help children learning</u> and to try to
       b   c
    <u>keep them</u> out of trouble.
        d

37. The Prime Minister angered many people <u>by the way</u> carrying
                                                   a
    on with <u>a</u> <u>golf</u> game for a couple of hours after he first <u>heard</u> the news
         b   c   d
    of a very tragic accident.

38. The practice of incarcerating juveniles in adult prisons for one day—hoping to scare <u>the delinquent</u>—<u>found favor</u> in Arkansas during the
   　　　　　　　　　　　　　　　　　　　　　a　　　　　　　　b
60's; numerous cases of abuse eventually surfaced there, <u>including with</u> <u>one involving</u> the death of Mr. Brown's 15-year-old son.
   　　　　　　　　　　　　　　　　　　　　　　　　　　c　　　　　　d

39. We need <u>to improve</u> our very poor English education program, but not everyone <u>in</u> our department <u>feel</u> <u>that way</u>.
   　　　　　　a　　　　　　　　　　　　　　　　　　　　　　　　　b　　　　　　　c　　d

40. With individuals and companies <u>lesser eager</u> to spend money <u>on</u> new computers now, <u>the resulting price wars</u> have made the PC business very difficult.
   　　　　a　　　　　　　　　　　　　　b　　　　　　　　　　c　　　　　　d

Practice Test 5

Directions: Questions 1-15 are incomplete sentences. Beneath each sentence, you will see four words or phrases, marked a, b, c, and d. Choose the **one** word or phrase that best completes the sentence.

1. This is ------- in college.

    a. that we wish to accomplish
    b. what you need to know to be successful
    c. where they want to spend
    d. when students try to achieve

2. I would rather ------- computer science in college.

    a. to have opted for
    b. for the teachers to teach
    c. that I had majored in
    d. studied

3. A class cannot be punished for what students think because ------- .

    a. every student is similar
    b. many students are like
    c. students are unlikely to truth
    d. all students do not think alike

4. According to Mr. Putin, Russia can help other countries launch ------- .

    a. space devices such as satellites
    b. rockets and likely stations
    c. space shuttles and alike vehicles
    d. many space stations such like Mir

5. As I shut the doors, I noticed a young boy standing there looking ------- .

    a. at me and very frightened
    b. sad and a little scared
    c. hungrily and a bit angrily
    d. into my eyes and very much willingly

6. At that university in America, not only was I the only Japanese, ------- .

   a. but I was the first student from Japan
   b. also was I the only international student
   c. but I was also the only foreigner
   d. as well as was I the only student from Asia

7. Everybody says Kiyoshi is doomed, since he ------- his dissertation mentor.

   a. is not a relationship with
   b. does not relate well to
   c. has no relation with whom
   d. established no relating to

8. I ------- to deal with the problem of extreme poverty when I was young.

   a. wouldn't rather have had
   b. would rather haven't had
   c. would rather not to have had
   d. would rather not have had

9. There has been very little ------- to their call for help.

   a. responsive
   b. responsibility
   c. responsiveness
   d. response

10. In a whiskey tasting class, you generally get to taste several whiskeys at once, which ------- .

    a. makes you to feel very happy
    b. gets you consider becoming a bartender
    c. helps you getting to learn the ropes
    d. lets you compare flavors

11. It is certainly cheaper for a university to ------- its own EFL program.

   a. come to us for help rather than to develop
   b. rather ask us to do the job for them than making
   c. cut corners than strictly following the regulations
   d. contract out the English program rather to start

12. My mother's desire was that I would have the great education that she wished ------- but didn't.

   a. she had had
   b. for myself
   c. not to spoil me
   d. I could get now

13. Ken is learning Indonesian ------- he will be able to speak it when he goes to Jakarta next year.

   a. hoping so much if
   b. so as not to achieving
   c. rather that
   d. so that

14. This town, where James lives, does not seem to have ------- , but this doesn't bother James.

   a. much history
   b. many good informations
   c. very a few good jobs
   d. only little amount of employment possibility

15. The artist painted a picture of three human figures in a line with their arms bent ------- .

   a. upward their heads
   b. upward-side down
   c. upwardly mobility
   d. upward

Directions: In questions 16-40 each sentence has four underlined words or phrases. The four underlined parts of the sentence are marked a, b, c, and d. Identify the **one** underlined word or phrase that must be changed in order for the sentence to be correct.

16. As if <u>to make up</u> <u>with</u> the time he couldn't spend with his family, Mr.
           a   b
    Gilmore now goes <u>on picnics</u> with his family <u>quite</u> regularly.
                        c   d

17. Because of the recently-adopted state policy of educating <u>even</u> the
                                                                       a
    least-motivated students, <u>any</u> longer <u>can a school have</u> <u>only</u> the best
                             b   c   d
    students do better to bring the average up.

18. Bob, who is <u>usually very</u> <u>gentle and reserved</u>, got very violent at the
                     a   b
    party last night; he <u>should</u> have had too much <u>to drink</u>.
                    c   d

19. The Church of the Holy Cross and its grammar school <u>were</u> the
                                                            a
    center of Richmond in the 1950s – a place of <u>refuge</u> for <u>much</u>
                                                     b   c
    neighborhood kids from <u>troubled homes</u>.
                              d

20. <u>Hundred</u> of magazines have claimed <u>that music</u>, especially <u>classical</u>
        a   b   c
    music, helps a baby's brain <u>develop faster</u>.
                               d

21. <u>In his book</u>, Dr. Marc Bolan acknowledged that <u>not every question</u>
       a   b
    <u>concerned</u> early dancing <u>could</u> be answered.
        c   d

22. In the Philippines, a nation <u>together</u> many languages, linguistics is a
                                                                           a
    discipline that should <u>be undertaken</u>, especially at the graduate level;
                                                          b
    however, <u>being</u> a non-commercial discipline, it attracts
                      c
    <u>very few students.</u>
             d

23. In the middle of the <u>weekly</u> meeting, Mr. Berry stood up and
                            a
    shouted, "I cannot <u>stand</u> <u>such an</u> unproductive discussion <u>like this</u>!"
                       b   c   d

24. Mark Farner was <u>so a good</u> singer that he had <u>numerous</u> fans when he
                       a   b
    was singing in a band <u>called</u> Grand Funk Railroad <u>in the early 70's.</u>
                           c   d

25. Most of the world's whiskeys used to <u>being</u> classified and <u>named</u> <u>by</u>
                                             a   b c
    the area or town <u>where</u> they were produced.
                   d

26. Mr. Mercury had a good life; he worked <u>on</u> construction jobs <u>on</u>
                                                a   b
    weekdays and <u>cost</u> weekends taking friends sailing to the Bahamas,
                   c
    only <u>charging them</u> for food and alcoholic beverages.
             d

27. <u>Owing to</u> the decrease <u>in</u> the number of school-age children, we have
        a   b
    decided to <u>relocate of</u> our school <u>outside</u> Japan.
                 c   d

28. Recently, researchers <u>probing beneath</u> the permanent ice shield
                                           a
    <u>around the South Pole</u> have located <u>in</u> as many as 76 lakes, including
            b   c
    one that is about 5,400 square miles, <u>comparable to</u> Lake Ontario.
                                                     d

29. Rocky's victory <u>over</u> the champion Apollo in the <u>recent heavyweight</u>
                      a   b
    boxing title match <u>caught</u> many people <u>in</u> surprise.
                       c   d

30. That new guitarist shows <u>to promise</u> <u>of becoming</u> one of the
                                 a   b
    <u>greatest rock musicians</u> of the <u>21st century</u>.
            c   d

31. The company offers, on <u>top</u> of many other benefits, several payment
                                a
    <u>option</u> to its employees in the <u>hope</u> of keeping them from being
     b   c
    headhunted by other <u>corporations</u>.
                              d

32. The <u>investigate</u> <u>of</u> a routine story by a detective <u>uncovers</u> many
        a   b   c
    secrets and networks of <u>corruption, conspiracy and deception</u>.
                                        d

33. The old professors finally decided <u>to take</u> special <u>carefulness</u> to
                                       a   b
    see that <u>all English majors will graduate</u> with <u>a certain competence</u> in
            c   d
    the English language.

34. Thinking that humility would be useful <u>on</u> dealing with office
    a
    politics, Mr. Yoshida never introduced himself <u>as</u> an able lawyer in
    b
    the multi-national law firm; <u>as a result,</u> many people came to ignore
    c
    him <u>as</u> a brainless loser.
    d

35. When I saw Karen in the second school play, <u>in which</u> she was
    a
    <u>virtually unrecognizable</u>, <u>not just physically</u>, <u>and</u> emotionally, I was
    b   c   d
    really intrigued.

36. When John learned he had failed math, he got <u>too</u> <u>upset</u> that he threw
                                                    a   b
    his math textbooks <u>into the air</u> and <u>howled like</u> a wolf.
                          c   d

37. According to the education committee, teachers who are not
    <u>capable of teaching</u> <u>will all</u> be dismissed <u>within</u> the <u>nearly six</u>
            a   b   c   d
    months.

38. In Hollywood, there are <u>so little</u> good roles <u>for</u> Asians <u>that</u> many
                              a   b   c
    Asian actors are forced to think about <u>a career change.</u>
                                               d

39. On January. 20, Al Bush, 44, received a <u>pardon</u> for a <u>1985</u> cocaine
                                              a   b
    possession conviction <u>for which</u> he had <u>serviced</u> one year in prison.
                              c   d

40. When making a speech in English, Takashi was so nervous that the
              ‾‾‾‾‾‾‾‾   ‾‾‾‾‾‾‾‾‾‾
                a   b
harder he tried to say something, very quiet he became.
‾‾‾‾‾‾   ‾‾‾‾‾‾‾‾‾‾
  c   d

Answers

必要に応じて本文中の解説を読んで復習ができるように、該当する問題番号を「☞」で示したので活用してほしい。(書き換えに関しては、代表的なものを記したまで。他に書き換え例がまったくないというわけではない。)

Practice Test 1

1. d (☞ 26)   2. b (☞ 1)   3. d (☞ 7)   4. d (☞ 32)   5. b (☞ 28)
6. b (☞ 25)   7. a (☞ 19)   8. b (☞ 34)   9. c (☞ 38)   10. a (☞ 14)
11. b (☞ 8)   12. c (☞ 9)   13. a (☞ 2)   14. c (☞ 33)   15. b (☞ 29)

16. a (most likely → more likely; ☞ 27)
17. b (contain → contains; ☞ 12)
18. d (itself → them; ☞ 13)
19. b (child → children; ☞ 23)
20. c (to smuggle → the smuggling of; ☞ 39)
21. b (different sort → a different sort; ☞ 10)
22. a (it the fact → the fact; ☞ 35)
23. c (asking → ask; ☞ 40)
24. a (seems to → seem to*; ☞ 17) *関係代名詞thatの先行詞は those twists of fate
25. b (both student → both students; ☞ 18)
26. b (manager → the manager; ☞ 21)
27. b (team → teams; ☞ 11)
28. c (relying barometer → reliable barometer; ☞ 4)
29. d (where are planes → where there are planes; ☞ 37)
30. c (to we → to us; ☞ 24)
31. d (the human history → human history; ☞ 20)
32. b (other cult → other cults; ☞ 15)
33. c (impact → an impact; ☞ 22)
34. b (slight → slightly; ☞ 6)
35. b (grand → grandly; ☞ 5)
36. a (it is → is; ☞ 36)
37. a (technology such as → technologies such as; ☞ 16)
38. c (temperate of → temperature of; ☞ 31)
39. b (some highly → some high; ☞ 3)
40. c (the public → those of the public; ☞ 30)

Practice Test 2

1. b (☞ 63)   2. a (☞ 72)   3. d (☞ 57)   4. c (☞ 54)   5. b (☞ 50)
6. a (☞ 53)   7. d (☞ 43)   8. d (☞ 51)   9. b (☞ 45)   10. c (☞ 71)
11. a (☞ 46)   12. d (☞ 59)   13. b (☞ 49)   14. a (☞ 41)   15. d (☞ 52)

16. a (thousands workers → thousand workers; ☞ 47)
17. c (where → which; ☞ 76)
18. c (would have → would; ☞ 44)
19. b (it is thought the children → the children; ☞ 55)
20. b (biology advance → advanced biology; ☞ 62)
21. a (which → in which; ☞ 79)
22. b (that → which; ☞ 78)
23. a (Locating → Located; ☞ 56)
24. b (which → where; ☞ 74)
25. c (its → her; ☞ 70)
26. b (since → for; ☞ 69)
27. b (weave into → woven into; ☞ 64)
28. b (said that → saying that; ☞ 58)
29. b (experiencing → experienced; ☞ 60)
30. d (before → since; ☞ 68)
31. b (excited tales → exciting tales; ☞ 61)
32. b (from → by; ☞ 65)
33. a (in that → that; ☞ 75)
34. b (available the lowest fares → the lowest fares available*; ☞ 66)
    *availableは単独でも名詞を後から修飾することが多い。
35. a (of which → of; ☞ 67)
36. d (plans of → plans to; ☞ 42)
37. a (who → whose; ☞ 80)
38. b (first → the first; ☞ 48)
39. b (for → ϕ /that; ☞ 77)
40. c (which → when; ☞ 73)

Practice Test 3

1. d (☞ 86)   2. c (☞ 91)   3. a (☞ 112)   4. b (☞ 116)   5. c (☞ 94)
6. c (☞ 99)   7. b (☞ 95)   8. c (☞ 102)   9. c (☞ 87)   10. a (☞ 97)
11. d (☞ 96)   12. a (☞ 89)   13. a (☞ 119)   14. d (☞ 107)   15. c (☞ 113)

16. a (The → A; ☞ 109)
17. a (most commoner → most common; ☞ 92)
18. a (like → with; ☞ 118)
19. c (year of 66 → age of 66; ☞ 106)
20. c (matters school → school matters; ☞ 85)
21. d (sum of enormous money → an enormous sum of money; ☞ 82)
22. a (would write → write; ☞ 90)
23. a (begin on → begin; ☞ 120)
24. d (individuals → individual; ☞ 115)
25. b (like → as; ☞ 100)
26. b (most best education → best education; ☞ 93)
27. a (the younger actresses resembled → did the younger actresses resemble; ☞ 88)
28. d (his old friend as → his old friend; ☞ 98)
29. b (restored be → be restored; ☞ 84)
30. b (even → even though; ☞ 105)
31. d (to → for; ☞ 110)
32. b (there → where; ☞ 81)
33. a (a great number of → a great deal of; ☞ 111)
34. a (done the research yet → already done the research; ☞ 114)
35. a (take advantage of → taking advantage of; ☞ 103)
36. d (aside cast → cast aside; ☞ 83)
37. d (that → as; ☞ 117)
38. d (not alike → unlike; ☞ 104)
39. d (of his own → as his own; ☞ 101)
40. c (of rewriting → rewriting; ☞ 108)

Practice Test 4

1. c (☞ 130) 2. b (☞ 152) 3. c (☞ 123) 4. a (☞ 157) 5. d (☞ 137)
6. a (☞ 121) 7. d (☞ 154) 8. d (☞ 132) 9. a (☞ 133) 10. d (☞ 142)
11. a (☞ 136) 12. c (☞ 153) 13. d (☞ 150) 14. c (☞ 148) 15. a (☞ 141)

16. c (10 Fahrenheit degree → 10 degrees Fahrenheit; ☞ 128)
17. c (on → to; ☞ 127)
18. c (to → and; ☞ 122)
19. d (world → the world; ☞ 144)
20. a (know to → know how to; ☞ 147)

21. b (beside → by; ☞ 125)
22. d (well faculty members → good faculty members; ☞ 140)
23. a (In spite → In spite of; ☞ 129)
24. b (to compare → comparing; ☞ 134)
25. a (out → out of; ☞ 158)
26. d (of → to; ☞ 160)
27. d (own imagination → their own imagination; ☞ 156)
28. c (base → basis; ☞ 151)
29. c (be interested in → interest; ☞ 146)
30. b (be concerned with → concern; ☞ 126)
31. a (given to → given; ☞ 139)
32. a (most acclaimed rock band → most acclaimed rock bands; ☞ 155)
33. c (enough long → long enough; ☞ 135)
34. c (to answer → answer; ☞ 138)
35. b (that → to; ☞ 159)
36. c (help children learning → help children learn; ☞ 143)
37. a (by the way → by; ☞ 124)
38. c (including with → including; ☞ 145)
39. c (feel → feels; ☞ 131)
40. b (lesser eager → less eager; ☞ 149)

Practice Test 5

1. b (☞ 198) 2. c (☞ 190) 3. d (☞ 161) 4. a (☞ 191) 5. b (☞ 197)
6. c (☞ 170) 7. b (☞ 183) 8. d (☞ 189) 9. d (☞ 193) 10. d (☞ 165)
11. a (☞ 171) 12. a (☞ 187) 13. d (☞ 179) 14. a (☞ 167) 15. d (☞ 184)

16. b (with → for; ☞ 164)
17. b (any → no; ☞ 168)
18. c (should → must; ☞ 176)
19. c (much → many; ☞ 166)
20. a (Hundred → Hundreds; ☞ 182)
21. c (concerned → concerning; ☞ 172)
22. a (together → with; ☞ 188)
23. d (like → as; ☞ 192)
24. a (so → such; ☞ 194)
25. a (being → be; ☞ 185)
26. c (cost → spent; ☞ 180)

27. c (relocate of → relocate; ☞ 173)
28. c (in as → as; ☞ 163)
29. d (in → by; ☞ 196)
30. a (to promise → promise; ☞ 177)
31. b (option → options; ☞ 175)
32. a (investigate → investigation; ☞ 199)
33. b (carefulness → care; ☞ 195)
34. a (on → in; ☞ 186)
35. d (and → but; ☞ 169)
36. a (too → so; ☞ 178)
37. d (nearly six → coming six/next six; ☞ 181)
38. a (so little → so few; ☞ 162)
39. d (serviced → served; ☞ 174)
40. d (very quiet → the quieter; ☞ 200)

音読でたたきこむTOEFL®テスト英文法　CD付き

2002年4月15日　1刷
2016年7月5日　7刷

著　者――生井健一
　　　　　©Kenichi Namai, 2002
発行者――南雲一範
発行所――株式会社 **南雲堂**
　　　　東京都新宿区山吹町361（〒162-0801）
　　　　電　話（03）3268-2384（営業部）
　　　　　　　（03）3268-2387（編集部）
　　　　ＦＡＸ（03）3260-5425（営業部）
　　　　振替口座　00160-0-46863
印刷所／日本ハイコム株式会社

Printed in Japan　〈検印省略〉
乱丁、落丁本はご面倒ですが小社通販係宛ご送付下さい。
送料小社負担にてお取替えいたします。

ISBN 978-4-523-26402-3　C0082〈1-402〉

音読でたたきこむTOEFL®テスト英文法

English Grammar Handbook for the TOEFL® Test

解答別冊集

英語の練習法

　英語の実力をつけるのに欠かせない基礎練習がリスニングと音読である。英語は言葉なのだから、音声を介したやり取りができるような練習をしないと本質を欠いた努力ということになってしまう。野球を例に取って考えてみよう。上達法を解説した本とルールブックばかりを何度も読み、内容をすべて覚えたとしても、実際にグランドに立ち、グローブやバットを手にして練習しなければ野球の上達はあり得ない。これと同様、日本式の英語筆記試験のための勉強のみをしていたのでは、到底「使える英語」（読み書きも含む）など獲得できない。リスニングと音読をして実際に英語そのものを練習しなければ何にもならないのである。

　日本人は、英語の読み書きはともかくリスニングとスピーキングが弱いと言われる。実際、多くの日本人が、「読み書きはどうにかなるが、リスニングとスピーキングは非常に難しい」と言う。昔ながらの学習法でしか英語に接してこなかった人たちには当然の結論であろう。しかし、正当な練習法にしたがって訓練を始めればすぐにこの結論が誤っていることがわかる。本当に難しいのはライティングとスピーキングで、リスニングとリーディングはそれに比べるとはるかに楽なのである。根拠は何か？前者はアクティブなスキルで、「通じるもの」をすべて自分で作り出さなければならないのに対し、後者は受身なので与えられたものを理解するだけでよい。ライティングとスピーキングの場合、簡単なメモ書きでも日常会話でも、生活に困らない程度にこなすには、瞬時に的確な判断ができるようでなければならない、これには熟練を要す。特にライティングは、スピーキングより正確さが要求され、ネイティブであっても苦手とする人が多いスキルである。実際、「英語ペラペラ」という帰国子女を指導する際、彼らの書く作文の稚拙さに唖然とさせられることがよくある。これに比べ、リスニングとリーディングは自分で作り出さなくていい分慣れるのも早い。そこで本格的に英語をやろうという人はまずリスニングとリーディングから入るとよい。しかし、ここで重要なのが、リスニングとリーディングをセットで練習するということ。以下で説明するが、リスニング抜きのリーディングは非常に効率が悪いのだ。

リスニングとリーディング

　リーディング練習の目標は、「長文読解」をふつうにこなせるようになること。長文とはいえ所詮短文の連なりを読むのだから、最初は、本書のような文

法事項が完結にまとめられた短文集を使うと良い。文法事項を理解して文章の意味がわかったら、それで満足せず、本書付属のCDを使ってきちんと聞き取れるかをチェックする。カタカナ英語に慣れきった耳には、ネイティブの発音は新鮮であるとともに難解かも知れない。しかし、本小冊子中の英文を見ながら、各単語の発音と各単語間の音の連結に耳を傾け、音を聞き取る練習をしよう。慣れてきたら英文を見ず、ディクテーションをしてみる。200しかないのだから、繰り返しディクテーションを行って単語の綴りも覚えてしまうとよい（TOEFLにおけるライティングでは、もちろん単語の綴りもチェックされる）。

　また、聞き取りを容易にするのに非常に有効なのが音読である。大体において聞き取れないものは、自分で言えないものである。よって、音読を繰り返して自分で言えるようにしてしまえば、聞き取れるようになるのだ。そこで、CDの音声に慣れたら、英文を見ながらそれをアメリカ人になったつもりで思い切り真似てみよう。後は回数の問題。できるだけ多く練習して、「英語の筋肉」を口の周りにつけてほしい。実際、英語に慣れ、頭の中で言いたい文章を完璧に作っても、「ろれつが回らず、相手に伝わらなかった」ということが多々ある。これを避けるには、音読あるのみ。つまり、真の語学はスポーツと同じなのである。

　音読が滑らかにできるようになったら、シャドウィングを始めよう。これは何も見ず、耳だけを頼りに音読する練習法である。CDをかけ、聞こえてきた音をすぐオウム返しすればよい。ふつうの音読の場合、情報は目から入ってくるのだが、シャドウィングの場合はそれが耳から入ってくるだけで、脳内の処理はまったく同じ。ネイティブのスピードに慣れながら、口の筋肉の鍛錬になる非常に効果的な練習法だ。しかしながら、「全文を暗記していないとオウム返しはできない」と誤解している英語学習者によく出会う。暗記はそれ自体良いことだが、シャドウィングに関しては関係ない。CDにおけるネイティブ・スピーカーとまったく同時に発音する必要はなく、聞こえてきたものをオウム返しするのだから、CDと練習者の音声間には1～2秒のギャップがあってしかるべきなのである。本来、シャドウィングというものは、初聴のものを使ってやるのだから、暗記などできない。しかし、同時通訳者になるための練習をしているのではないので、音読をしっかりこなした後、ネイティブのスピードに慣れるための練習として行えばよいのである。

　このような練習をした後で黙ってCDに耳を傾けると、当然のことながらすべてが聞き取れる。また、きちんと意味を理解した上で音読とシャドウィングの練習を行うので、数をこなせばこなすほど、英語を英語の語順で理解できるようになってくる。（稀に音声と意味を完全に切り離して練習してしまう英語

学習者に出会うが、その場合、意図的に意味をイメージしながら音読とシャドウィングをする必要があろう。）そして、これが、同じパッシブ・スキルであるリーディングの上達に大きくものを言うのである。

　日本の大学入試などにはふつう長文読解問題が出るが、TOEFLに比べると与えられる時間がとても長い。これは、日本語に訳してから理解するという日本の学校英語教育を反映しているからであろう。よって、こういう英語教育しか受けていないふつうの日本人にはTOEFLのリーディング・セクションは時間が足らず、ほとんどの場合歯が立たないということになる。確かに貧弱な語彙力の問題もあるが、必要以上に時間をかけて語順がまったく違う日本語にいちいち置き換えないと理解できないというのでは、日本人が得意であるとされる「読み」のスキルも、「使える」という基準からすると「非常に怪しい」と言わざるを得ない。

　しかしながら、リスニングの練習を積んだ者は、リーディングのスピードも速い。リスニングにおいて英文を理解するということは、英語を英語の語順で理解することに他ならないからだ。そして、これができるようになれば、英文を読解するときも必然的に英語の語順で行えるようになる。こうなれば、TOEFLのリーディングにだって十分太刀打ちできる。つまり、リスニング力を鍛えることによって、「使える」リーディング力もつくというわけだ。まさに一石二鳥。これに対し、英語を英語の語順で理解する訓練をリーディングのみでするのは容易ではない。わからないときはたやすく前に戻れる。漢文を読むように、強引に日本語に置き換えることだってできる。「英語の語順で理解するぞ」と意気込んでも、つい戻ってしまう。一方、リスニングでは、聞き逃したら最後、戻りたくても戻れない。それに言葉は本来聞いて話すものなのだから、最初からリスニングの練習に力を入れるのは当然のことなのである。

文法とCDの使い方

　文法項目の説明ばかりやたらと得意な人がいる。それはそれでいいのだが、にも関わらず、実際に英語を聞いたり、話したりすることは苦手である、となると考えものである。文法は、スポーツにおける「コツ」のようなもので、理屈を理解しても、本当に使えるようになるには、やはり練習が必要なのである。練習に練習を重ね、コツを身体に叩き込み、いざというときは自然に身体が動くというようにならなければならない。仕事や留学先で英会話をしたり、英文を書くときに、いちいち文法を考えていたら、日常生活にも支障をきたすであろう。よって、ある文法項目の理屈がわかったら実際にそれが使われている英

文を、まずは 1 つ覚えてしまうとよい。後は会話でも日記でも何でもいいので、積極的にそれを応用して使うこと。また、多読、多聴することによってインプットを増やし、その項目に十分慣れるように努力する。こうして、考えなくても自然に文法を操れるようになるまで訓練する。

　本書の「はじめに」のところに書いたが、実際に使われる文法項目などそれほど多くない。付属のCDには本書の200の例文が収録されているので、各文法項目の説明を理解したら、この小冊子とポータブルCDプレーヤーを常に持ち歩き、空いた時間をすべてつぎ込んで、上に書いたようにリスニング、ディクテーション、音読、シャドウィングをして例文ごと頭に叩き込んでいただきたい。後は、実際に使ってみること。毎日英語で日記でもつけ、新しく覚えた文法項目を積極的に活用する。その際、英語のよくわかる人に添削してもらえたら理想的だ。このようにして、各文法項目が身に付けば、TOEFLのライティングに対しても非常に有利になる。また、TOEFLの文法セクション対策としては、これと同時に何度も本書の問題（パート1とパート3で400題ある）を解き、瞬間的にどれがどういう理屈で答になるのかが言えるようにする。後は過去問を数多く解き、同時に語彙と成句の獲得に努力すれば、文法セクションはあなたの楽勝セクションになるであろう。

まとめ

　本書は英文法のハンドブックであるのだが、結局のところ、文法だけの勉強などあり得ないということだ。理屈を理解するのはもちろん必要だが、それと同時にリスニングや音読を通して、それをいかに身に付けるかが重要なのである（これは語彙力増強にも言える）。日本語を話すときを考えてみてほしい。文法など考えることなく、自然に文章が作れるではないか。大人になってから英語を獲得しようというのだから、最初は文法書を頼りに英語のルールを学ばなければならない。しかし、それと同時にその知識が当たり前のものになるまで、練習を繰り返すことのほうが大切なのである。本書を読んでTOEFLが問うアメリカの学校文法を理解し、付属のCDを使ってリスニングや音読をこなす。そして、すべてを体得したと思ったら、より高度なものにどんどん挑戦していってほしい。本屋にはCDおよび解説付の生きた英語の教材が山とある。ビデオやDVD教材だってあふれている。自分の実力や趣味にあったものを選んで、ディクテーション、音読、シャドウィング等をたっぷり行い、真の実力をつけていただきたい。

　それにしても、英語教材にこれほど恵まれた国はない。衛星放送だって当た

り前の時代で、24時間英語漬けの生活も簡単に実現できる。こういう状況下で使える英語が獲得できないというのは、詰まるところ、やる気の問題ではないか。何、やる気だけはある？では、何も心配することはなさそうだ。Good luck!

1. The Japanese wolf was thought to be a **dangerous animal** and was hunted to extinction.
   ニホンオオカミは危険な動物であると思われ、乱獲の結果絶滅してしまった。

2. Despite some **local protests**, the National University of Singapore is admitting more foreign students.
   地元に抗議があるにも関わらず、シンガポール国立大学は外国人学生の数を増やしている。

3. The scientist's **initial interest** was in what she thought to be a simple chemical reaction.
   簡単な化学反応にすぎないと思っていたものに科学者は最初興味を持っていた。

4. In the end, we succeeded in making a film out of the science fiction, while still managing to make it feel **believable**.
   我々は最終的にそのSFからいかにもありそうな話の映画を作り出すことに成功した。

5. We should check **carefully** that there are no careless mistakes before we turn in our exams.
   試験を提出する前に、ケアレスミスがないように注意深くチェックするべきだ。

6. We would like to offer a **significantly more sophisticated** cruise experience, from upgraded cuisine to curtains and double beds in the berths.
   ワンランク上の食事から寝台室のカーテンとダブルベッドに至るまで、はるかに洗練されたクルーズ体験を提供したいと思っております。

7. During the interview, the author's legs were crossed, and much of the time **so were her arms**, as if she was shielding herself from public prying.
   インタビューの間作家は足を組み、しょっちゅう腕組みもして、あたかも公衆の詮索から自らを守っているようだった。

8. The announcement that scientists have made the first reading of the human genetic code marks the next major step in the project, since scientists **finished** decoding the human genome **last June**.
   科学者がヒトの遺伝子コードの最初の読み取りに成功したという発表は、プロジェクトにおける次の大きなステップを印すものである。というのも、去年の6月に科学者はヒトゲノムの解析を終わらせているからだ。

9. In his nervous gestures, his discomfort with the situation clearly **manifested itself**.
その状況が不快であることは、彼のいらいらしたジェスチャーにはっきり表れていた。

10. **One type** of computer program that has been developed at the institute is an excellent machine translation program.
その研究所で開発されたコンピュータ・プログラムの1つのタイプは優秀な機械翻訳プログラムである。

11. I love these **three collections** of folk songs produced by Ken Marcus in the 1970's.
僕は1970年代にケン・マーカスによってプロデュースされたこれら3つのフォークソング・コレクションが大好きだ。

12. At least **three** out of every four Ph.D. students at that university **fail** to graduate.
その大学では、少なくとも4人に3人の博士課程の学生が卒業できない。

13. Unlike most of his colleagues, **the biology professor** still **appears** to be in good health.
生物学教授は、彼の同僚のほとんどとは違い、まだ健康そうである。

14. Native to Southeast Asia, **that species** of lizard **is** found in wet regions.
東南アジアに特有であるそのトカゲの種は、湿地帯に見られる。

15. In the Department of Physics, as in **other departments** at the university, students are expected to write a graduation thesis of a publishable quality.
その大学の他学科同様物理学科でも、学会誌に載るくらいの卒論を書くことが学生に求められている。

16. They were unable to attend the meeting for **various reasons**.
彼らはさまざまな理由でミーティングに出席できなかった。

17. Her **knowledge** of three languages and economics **helps** her greatly in her work.
3ヶ国語と経済学を知っていることが、仕事において彼女の大きな助けになっている。

18. Before you call it a day, you must paint **both sides** of this wall.
仕事を終える前に、この壁の両面を塗らないといけないよ。

19. One of the typical metropolitan cities often used in market research is **Columbus, Ohio, the capital of the state**.
市場調査によく使われる典型的な大都市の1つがオハイオ州の州都コロンバスである。

20. **Forensic linguistics** is a relatively new field, but it has already attracted many researchers because of its promising future.
犯罪言語学は比較的新しい分野であるが、発展の見込みがあるためすでに多くの研究者が生まれている。

21. Dr. Noguchi tried to find the cause of yellow fever in the early 20th century, in **the decades preceding** the advent of the electron microscope.
    野口博士は20世紀の初頭、電子顕微鏡が出現する前の時代に、黄熱病の原因を見つけようとした。

22. His reports are always dubious, because he never gets information from any reliable source but instead from **a** much more obscure secondary **source**.
    彼のレポートはいつも疑わしい。というのも、彼は決して信頼できる筋からではなく、代わりにずっと怪しい二流の筋から情報を得ているからだ。

23. The Peterson Home for **Boys** is one of the best reform schools in the nation.
    ピーターソン・ホーム・フォー・ボーイズは国中で最も優秀な少年院の1つである。

24. The musicians suggested that the scores be sent **to them** by special delivery so that they could get to work on the project immediately.
    音楽家たちは直ちにそのプロジェクトに取り掛かれるよう、楽譜を速達で受け取ることを主張した。

25. Although Miss White gave a definitive answer, her students looked for **their own** creative solutions.
    ホワイト先生は最終的な答を教えたが、生徒たちは自分たちの創造的な解決策を探すことにした。

26. Karen is a very warm person, and **it** is that aspect of her character **that** has enabled her to get her friends to trust her with intimate stories about their lives.
    カレンはとても心が温かく、彼女の友達が自分たちの生活における個人的な話まで彼女にしてしまうのは、彼女のそういうところによるものである。

27. Carbon dioxide and other greenhouse gases from human activities are **more likely to have caused** the one-degree rise in global temperature since 1950 than most other possible causes.
    1950年以来地球気温が1度上昇したのは、人々の営みから出される二酸化炭素とその他の温室効果を持つ気体が原因で、他に考えられる理由のほとんどのせいではなさそうだ。

28. Many people expect the economy to be better off in six months **than it is today**.
    景気は6ヶ月後には現在よりよくなっているだろうと、多くの人が思っている。

29. Last week's economics lecture was a comparison of the economy today and **that of 1990**, the last time the United States suffered a recession.
    先週の経済学の講義は、今日の景気と1990年、つまりアメリカが最後に不況を経験した年のそれとの比較であった。

30. Despite the general slowdown, which dragged down its shares more than **those of most of its rivals**, the computer company has managed to strongly outsell many of them.
そのコンピュータ会社は、全般的な景気後退でほとんどのライバル会社よりも株価を下げたが、売上では大きく差をつけた。

31. As we all know, **automobile insurance** is cheaper in America than in Japan.
我々みんなが知っているように、自動車保険は日本よりアメリカのほうが安い。

32. If I **were** a college student, I **would study** very hard and try to gain as much knowledge as possible.
もし僕が大学生だったら、一生懸命勉強してできる限りの知識を得ようとするのに。

33. We will surely reach a decision in the next meeting if the incompetent chairperson **does not** show up.
もし無能な議長が来なければ、我々は次のミーティングできっと何らかの決定を見るだろう。

34. This information might prove useful **if** the need ever arises to sue that incompetent lawyer.
万一あの無能な弁護士を訴えることになったら、この情報は役に立つかもしれない。

35. The citizens of that country do not even **appreciate their freedom**, which they simply take for granted.
あの国の人たちは、自由を単に当たり前のものとみなし、自由であることをありがたいとさえ思っていない。

36. **The visiting English professor from a very prestigious university in America told** us to watch as many English programs as possible on satellite TV in order to improve listening comprehension.
アメリカの超名門大学から来た英文学の客員教授は、リスニング力を増すために、衛星放送でできるだけ多くの英語番組を見なさいと私たちに言った。

37. **There** has **been** a decrease in the importation of foreign cars.
外国車の輸入に減少が生じた。

38. The English teacher complimented one of her students **for knowing** more English words than she herself did.
英語教員は、自分より多くの英単語を知っていたので、教え子の一人を誉めた。

39. During the 1980's, **the teaching of** biology at the university was much more effective than it is now.
1980年代の間、その大学での生物学教育は今よりもずっと効果的であった。

40. With regard to the possibility of transferring to another school, first **consult** the international student advisor.
転校の可能性については、まずインターナショナル・スチューデント・アドバイザーに相談しなさい。

41. Go over your answers as many times as possible **to make sure** that you don't make any careless mistakes.
    ケアレスミスをしないようにできるだけ多く繰り返して答を見直しなさい。

42. Freddie Mercury's reputation as a great rock singer rests on his ability **to give** emotional depth to his songs.
    偉大なロックシンガーとしてのフレディー・マーキュリーの名声は、歌に情熱的な深みを持たせる彼の能力によるものである。

43. The State Department urged American citizens **not to travel** to that country, warning that unrest and violence could break out at any time.
    国務省は、社会的不安定ひいては暴動がいつでも起こり得ると警告を出し、アメリカ市民にその国へは行かないよう促した。

44. I know students are supposed to study hard, but I don't think we **should** necessarily force them to do so.
    学生が一生懸命勉強するべきであるのはわかっているが、必ずしも我々が彼らに無理強いするべきだと私は思わない。

45. Scientists had expected to find about 100,000 genes per person; instead, they found about 30,000—only **twice as many as** a fly has, and 10,000 more than a worm.
    科学者は1人の人間につき約10万の遺伝子が見つかるだろうと予測していたが、約3万しかないことがわかった。これは、ハエの2倍、またミミズより1万多いに過ぎない。

46. When we talk to someone on the telephone, we tend to concentrate **twice as hard** on the conversation.
    電話で人と話すとき、我々は会話に2倍集中する傾向にある。

47. The number of air travelers in the nation climbed nearly 10 percent between 1995 and 2000 to **200 million**.
    国内における飛行機の旅客者の数は1995年と2000年の間に10パーセント増えて2億人になった。

48. Flight 852 for San Francisco is now boarding at **Gate Five**.
    サンフランシスコ行き852便は、現在第5ゲートで搭乗中です。

49. I have an appointment to see the professor on **the first** of the month.
    私はその月の1日に教授に会う約束がある。

50. Dorothy Stratten was a young, beautiful, and **talented** model when she was killed at the age of 20.
    20の若さで殺されたとき、ドロシー・ストラットンは若くて美しい、才能のあるモデルだった。

51. The professor of molecular biology demanded from his graduate students **an orderly experiment**, **a publishable paper**, and **hard work**.
    分子生物学の教授は、きちんとした実験、学会誌に掲載されるくらいの論文、そして勤勉さを大学院生たちに要求した。

52. Edward is **a physics teacher**, **a rock guitarist**, and **a private detective**.
    エドワードは物理教師、ロックギタリスト、そして私立探偵である。

53. Mr. Mercury **entered** the classroom, **stood up** in front of the students, and **announced** that he was postponing the exam scheduled for that day.
    マーキュリー先生は教室に入り、生徒たちの前に立ち、その日に予定されていた試験を延期すると発表した。

54. The final examination will be scored and evaluated by all the faculty members.
    期末試験はすべての教員によって採点され、評価される。

55. **Finishing** the paper tonight, **John** plans to mail it to the journal tomorrow.
    ジョンは、今晩その論文を終えて、明日学会誌に送る予定だ。

56. **Accustomed** to getting up early, **the new teacher** found it easy to teach 8 o'clock classes.
    早起きに慣れているので、その新任教師は8時のクラスを教えるのを苦にしなかった。

57. **A true believer in UFOs, Mr. Adams** has moved to England in the hope of meeting aliens, who he believes are responsible for all those crop circles.
    UFOの真の信者であるアダムズ氏はエイリアンに会いたくてイングランドに引っ越した。というのも、氏はエイリアンがミステリー・サークルを作っていると信じているからだ。

58. From 1967 to 1971, Jim Morrison was at the height of his singing career, **recording** his six most famous albums.
    1967年から1971年の間、ジム・モリソンは歌手として全盛期にあり、後の最も有名な6つのアルバムをレコーディングしている。

59. **A foreign student in Florida**, upon **leaving** his dormitory for class, immediately got bitten by a mosquito.
    あるフロリダの留学生は、授業に行くために寮を出たとたんに蚊に喰われた。

60. America has avoided two recessions in recent years because of the economic growth **provided by** new technologies.
    新しいテクノロジーによってもたらされた経済成長のおかげで、アメリカは近年、不況を2度避けることができた。

61. Tom did a presentation for his physics class, hoping to see Mrs. Johnson's **approving** smile, but unfortunately, she was sleeping throughout the presentation.
    トムはジョンソン先生の満足げな笑顔を期待して物理のクラスでの発表を行ったが、残念なことに、先生は発表の間中居眠りしていた。

62. The **parked** cars were all severely vandalized by juvenile delinquents in the neighborhood.
    停まっていた車はすべて近所の不良たちにひどく壊されてしまった。

63. The new airport opened almost three years ago in the hope that **passengers could be lured away** from the increasingly congested international airport nearby.
   どんどん混雑がひどくなる近隣の国際空港から利用者を引き寄せようと、その新しい飛行場がオープンされてもう3年になる。

64. During the last 10 years, only six new runways **have been added** at large hub airports in the nation.
   ここ10年の間、国内の大きなハブ空港にたった6つしか新しい滑走路が追加されていない。

65. The student suspects **were identified by** some classmates as anti-social troublemakers.
   生徒である容疑者たちは、クラスメートに反社会的問題児であるとみなされていた。

66. **Any teacher capable of** saying such a thing before students probably shouldn't have become a teacher in the first place.
   生徒たちの前でそんなことが言える教師は、最初から教師になどなるべきではなかったのだろう。

67. The detective was initially intrigued by medical reports he found in the files of **what was supposed to be** a minor divorce lawsuit.
   探偵は小さな離婚訴訟になるであろうと思われていた一件のファイルの中に見つけた医者の報告書に最初興味をそそられていた。

68. The priest first met the college students in their childhood, and **since** then, he **has given** them moral support.
   牧師がその大学生たちに会ったのは彼らがまだ子供のころであったが、それ以来彼らに精神的援助をしてきた。

69. The president has been on the line **for more than an hour**; something bad must have happened.
   社長は1時間以上も電話に出ている。何か悪いことが起こったに違いない。

70. **Norma Arnold** says individual attention has worked for **her** fifth-grade daughter and seventh-grade son.
   ノーマ・アーノルドによると、1人1人に注意を払うことが、彼女の5年生の娘と7年生の息子にはよかったのだという。

71. **Brian Setzer**'s rockabilly songs, most of which are reminiscent of Elvis Presley, established **him** as a leading American singer in the 1980's.
   ブライアン・セッツァーのロカビリー曲は、そのほとんどがエルビス・プレスリーを彷彿させるもので、彼に1980年代におけるアメリカを代表する歌手という地位をもたらした。

72. The researchers are happy to be at the institute, where they have **an opportunity** to conduct unprecedented scientific research.
   研究者たちは、先例のない科学リサーチを行う機会が得られるその研究所にいられて幸せである。

73. This story depicts two boys who lost their innocence **at a time**—the mid-1970's—**when** Japan was losing its own innocence.
    この物語は、1970年代半ば、つまり日本が純潔さを失っていった時代に純潔さを失った2人の少年を描いている。

74. In a **world where** heroes are often in short supply, the story of Rudy is an inspirational reminder of the power of the human spirit.
    よくヒーロー不足が指摘される世界において、「ルーディー」の物語は、人間の精神力を思い起こさせ、やる気にさせてくれる。

75. This is a true story about friendship **that** runs deeper than blood.
    これは、血縁より深い友情についての物語である。

76. The lawyer visited St. Mark's Church, **which** to him **had represented** a haven throughout so much of his childhood.
    弁護士は、自分にとって子供時代のほとんどを通じての避難所とも言える場所であったセント・マーク教会を訪れた。

77. These are **the rules and regulations all the members of this health club must abide by**.
    これが、このヘルスクラブの会員すべてが従わなければならないルールと規則である。

78. She left early, **which** was smart, since the party got so wild that the neighbors eventually called the police.
    彼女は早く帰ったが、それは賢い選択だった。というのも、パーティーは非常に荒れて、隣人がついには警察を呼ぶまでに至ったからだ。

79. The political leader is still chasing the ideal of a democratic and free society **in which** all persons will live together in harmony and with equal opportunities.
    その政治的指導者は、万人が仲よく平等な機会を持って一緒に暮らすという民主的自由社会の理想を今でも追い求めている。

80. While the students were sitting in the cafeteria, they noticed a girl eating in a corner booth – a girl **whose** face they could never forget.
    カフェテリアに座っている間、その学生たちはある女の子が角のブースで食事しているのに気がついた。彼らには決して忘れられない顔であった。

81. One of my favorite scenes in the movie is **where** Rudy arrives at the University of Notre Dame without even applying to the university.
    その映画の私の大好きなシーンの1つは、ルーディーが願書も出さずにノートルダム大学に到着するところである。

82. The professor let us copy for our movie some of his framed degrees and **other memorabilia of his long career**.
    教授は、我々の映画のために、額に入った学位と彼の長い経歴における他の記念の品のコピーを作らせてくれた。

83. He offered **his heartfelt sympathy** at the death of her mother.
    彼は、彼女の母親の死に際して心から同情した。

84. Rocky, one of the best motion pictures of the 1970's, **was written by** the actor Sylvester Stallone.
    1970年代最高の映画の１つであるロッキーは、俳優シルベスター・スタローンによって書かれた物語である。

85. My father's company does random testing of its products for **quality control**.
    父の会社は、品質管理のために製品をランダムにテストしている。

86. For the election scheduled for **next month**, the majority of voters **will be** independents.
    来月予定されている選挙では、投票者の大部分を無党派層が占めるだろう。

87. Hideki **asked** the professor whether or not she **knew** the word "competence."
    秀樹は教授に"competence"という単語を知っているか尋ねた。

88. **Not once**, in any of these amusement parks, **did we have** to compete with big crowds.
    これらのどの遊園地でも、１度たりとも混雑にもまれる必要はなかった。

89. Only with a bank loan **will he be** able to buy a house.
    銀行からのローンによってのみ、彼は家を買えるだろう。

90. It is **obligatory** that a foreign student see the international student advisor before signing up for any class.
    外国人学生は、どのクラスの科目登録をするにも、まずインターナショナル・スチューデント・アドバイザーに会わなくてはならない。

91. The professor suggested that the lazy student stop coming to her class because he wasn't studying at all.
    教授は、その怠惰な学生がまったく勉強していないので、授業に来るなと言った。

92. Noting a racial remark in a speech by a famous comedian, John said to himself, "That is **one of the most foolish statements I have ever heard**."
    有名なコメディアンによるスピーチの中に人種差別的な発言を聞いたとき、ジョンは「あれは今まで聞いた中で最も馬鹿らしいステートメントの１つだ」と独り言を言った。

93. The actress is beautiful, and she uses her beauty **to the fullest**.
    その女優は美しく、そして自分の美を十分に利用している。

94. **Good coaches know** their sports thoroughly.
    よいコーチは、自分のスポーツを完全に把握している。

95. **Two atoms of hydrogen combine** with one of oxygen to form water.
    水素原子2つが酸素原子1つと結びついて水を作る。

96. Jimi Hendrix attempted to prove that **rock music was** a form of art.
    ジミ・ヘンドリクスは、ロック音楽が芸術の1形態であることを証明しようとした。

97. Many business people in Japan are now learning communicative English in order to **remain competitive**.
    今、日本の多くのビジネス人が、競争力を保とうとしてコミュニカティブ・イングリッシュを習っている。

98. The photographer often **makes his family members his subjects**.
    その写真家は、しばしば自分の家族を被写体にする。

99. Hard work will continue to **make possible the realization of his numerous dreams**.
    勤勉が、彼の数え切れない夢をかなえ続けるだろう。

100. My solutions to the problems were **the same as** the teacher's.
     その問題の私の解決法は、先生のと同じだった。

101. These chemistry textbooks are **the same** size **as** those physics ones.
     これらの化学の教科書は、あれらの物理の教科書と同じサイズである。

102. Mudslides and collapsed buildings have effectively blocked the roads, **keeping** needed aid **from reaching** the thousands of people left homeless by the big earthquake.
     泥流と崩壊した建物が事実上道をふさいでしまい、大地震でホームレスになった何千もの人々に必要な援助が届くのを妨げていた。

103. John is now at a point in his life where he is looking forward **to retiring and playing golf**.
     ジョンは、今や引退してゴルフをすることを実際に楽しみにできる年齢である。

104. **Unlike** many tourist attractions, this one is like nature's amusement park and will surely blow your mind.
     多くの観光名所とは違い、これは自然の遊園地であり、きっとあなたはびっくりするだろう。

105. **Even though** we think the Asian economic crisis ended in 1999, there remain signs that indicate otherwise.
     アジアの経済危機は1999年に終わったと我々は思っているが、そうではないと示唆する印がまだ見られる。

106. Those young gangsters, who at that time had been from 16 to 18 **years of age**, never made it past the age of 30.
     当時年齢が16から18であったあの若いギャングメンバーたちは、30まで生きることはなかった。

107. We have **rarely** seen such an effective teacher as she has proven herself to be.
彼女は実践して見せてくれたが、我々は彼女ほど効果的な教育をする教師をめったに見たことがない。

108. The Linguistics Department **is in serious need of** experts in formal semantics and computational linguistics.
言語学科は、形式意味論とコンピュータ言語学の専門家を非常に必要としている

109. **A number of** universities in that country are already offering computational linguistics programs on the web.
その国の多くの大学が、すでにウェブ上でコンピュータ言語学のプログラムを提供している。

110. Thomas Edison was **well known for** his love of books when he was little.
トーマス・エジソンは、子供のとき、無類の本好きであったことで有名だ。

111. They handled the chemical with **a great deal of caution**, since it was known to be very explosive.
彼らは、その化学薬品をとても注意深く扱った。というのも、その薬品はとても爆発しやすいことで知られていたからだ。

112. This drug is effective, but it takes a long time to **act on** the pain.
この薬は効果的であるが、痛みに効くのに長い時間がかかる。

113. **That Korean student**, along with others from Taiwan, is to visit the nursery to entertain the children there.
あの韓国人学生は、台湾からの他の学生たちとともに、託児所に行って子供たちを喜ばせる予定だ。

114. The computer company has **already** notified most of the 3,000 people who will lose their jobs as part of a cost-cutting campaign.
そのコンピュータ会社は、コスト削減キャンペーンの一環として仕事を失う3,000人のほとんどにすでに通達している。

115. Bored with the lecture, the student dreamed up a classroom prank, more for diversion than **any other reason**.
講義に飽きて、その学生は教室でのいたずらを思いついたが、気晴らしのためという理由以外の何物でもなかった。

116. The practice of bribing that went on between the two companies **appears to have peaked** about two years ago.
両社における贈収賄の慣習は、約2年前がピークであったようである。

117. The single most important change for the English Program will be to hire as **quickly as** possible only teachers who are capable of speaking the language.
英語学科にとっての最も重要な改革は、できるだけはやく、英語を話せる教師のみを雇うことであろう。

118. Here, **as in Japan**, reactions to the film were far from subdued.
日本と同様ここでも、その映画に対する反応は静かなものなんかではなかった。

119. How to be more competitive is a question that is normally **associated with** men.
いかにより競争力を持てるようになれるかというのは、通常男性のものとされる問題である。

120. When the professor made two contradictory remarks, students **began to question** the credibility of her lecture.
教授が２つの矛盾する発言をしたとき、学生たちは彼女の講義の信頼性を疑問視し始めた。

121. Tom is one of the students who will **benefit financially from** Mrs. Taylor's generous donation to the university.
トムは、テーラー夫人からの大学への気前よい寄付によって、経済的に恩恵を被るであろう学生の１人である。

122. Interactive toys are likely to replace the more important interaction **between children and caring adults**.
インタラクティブなおもちゃが、より重要な、子供と世話を施す大人の間のふれ合いに取って代わりそうである。

123. Family members of those still missing had to speak at an emotional news conference, expressing **both their sadness and anger**.
未だに行方不明である人達の家族は、感情いっぱいの記者会見で話をしなければならず、悲しみと怒りの両方を打ち明けた。

124. The government is pushing universities to ride the globalization wave **by recruiting foreign teachers and admitting foreign students**.
政府は大学に、外国人教師を雇い、外国人学生を入学させることで、国際化の波に乗るよう働きかけている。

125. It is admirable that Karen wishes to solve all the problems **by herself**, but it might be better if she asked her teacher for help.
すべての問題を自分自身で解決したいというのは賞賛に値するが、カレンは先生に助けを求めたほうがよいのかもしれない。

126. Mr. Mercury **was** very **concerned about** the whereabouts of his cat.
マーキュリー氏は、彼の猫がどこにいるのかをとても気にしていた。

127. We expect new factors, such as classes offered through the Internet, to be reflected in our annual best universities survey; for now, however, the same names continue **to dominate** the top places.
我々は、インターネットで提供される授業というような新しい要素を、毎年のベスト・ユニバーシティ調査に加味していく予定である。しかし、現在のところ、同じ大学名が上位を独占し続けている。

128. The freezing point of water is **32 degrees Fahrenheit**.
水の氷点は、華氏32度である。

129. **Despite** the director's initial fears concerning the graphic nature of some of his film's scenes, the ratings board gave the movie a lenient R rating without a single cut.
監督は最初、自分の映画の数シーンの描写が生々しいので心配していたが、レーティング委員会は、1つのカットもなしに、その映画に寛大なRレーティングを与えた。

130. Teachers **differed** tremendously **in** how competently they taught their subjects in class.
教員は、どれくらいうまく担当科目をクラスで教えているかという点において千差万別であった。

131. In order to improve efficiency, we must find a solution to **each** major **problem** in our company.
能率を上げるために、我が社における大きな問題のそれぞれに対する解決策を見つけねばならない。

132. I had no idea Karen and you were that fond of **each other**.
カレンと君がそれほどお互いを気に入っているとはまったく知らなかった。

133. Neither Hillary nor **her friends are** going to class today.
ヒラリーも彼女の友達も、今日は授業に出ない。

134. She is a very talented actress whom you enjoy watching.
彼女は見ていて楽しい、とても才能のある女優だ。

135. Politicians, professors, and ugly buildings all get respectable if they last **long enough**.
政治家と大学教授と醜い建築物は、長くもてば、みんな尊敬の対象になる。

136. At their very **first encounter**, the banker deliberately mispronounced the detective's name as a slight put-down.
初めて会ったときに、銀行家は少し馬鹿にして探偵の名前をわざと間違えて発音した。

137. Our meetings always drone on into the night, crawling **from** one excruciatingly minor administrative detail to another.
我々のミーティングは、苦痛なほどつまらない管理的詳細から詳細へとのろのろ進み、いつも夜まで続いてしまう。

138. For more than a year, Miss White has been trying to **get** her shy students to **voice** their opinions in class.
ホワイト先生は、シャイな教え子たちにクラスで意見を言わせる努力を1年以上している。

139. This movie is not an indictment of the university system, but it does question the unchecked power that is **given to** people who may abuse it.
この映画は大学システムの告発ではないが、乱用しかねない者に与えられる制限なしの権力についてはっきり疑問を投げかけている。

140. The detective finally revealed to her that with **good intentions**, he had tried to prevent something terrible from happening there to a woman he cared for, only to hasten the tragedy.
よかれと思って、好きな女にひどいことが起こるのを防ごうと頑張ったのだが、結局悲劇を早めただけだったと、ついに探偵は彼女に明かした。

141. I **have no idea** what the speaker meant by the opening remark in his speech.
演説者がスピーチの最初の発言で何が言いたかったのか、私には見当もつかない。

142. It was while lying on her sofa that she first **heard** about another patient whose story seemed larger than life.
彼女が、まさかと思うような話を持つ他の患者について最初に聞いたのは、ソファに横たわっているときだった。

143. This is the approach that we recommend to help students **cope with growing demands**, academically and socially.
学問の上でも社会においても増えてきている要求に学生たちがうまく対処する手助けとして、我々が勧めるアプローチはこれである。

144. No other city **in the world** has ever created a billboard environment quite like Kabukicho's.
世界のどの都市も、歌舞伎町のような宣伝看板の環境を生み出していない。

145. Following the publication of his first paper in a major scientific journal, the researcher has seven other projects pending, **including** one about animal communication.
主要な科学ジャーナルに最初の論文を掲載したのに続き、その研究者は他に動物のコミュニケーションについてのプロジェクトを含む7つの未完成プロジェクトを抱えている。

146. Students who **are interested in** advanced physics should come to see me.
上級物理に興味のある学生は、私に会いに来ること。

147. Jane was working 90 hours a week as a freelance technical writer, not because she needed the money but because **she didn't know how to say no**.
ジェーンは週に90時間フリーのテクニカル・ライターとして働いていたが、お金が必要だったからではなく、断り方を知らなかったからだ。

148. The climate here is **less mild** than that of California.
ここの気候は、カリフォルニアのそれより穏やかでない。

149. The new anti-crime law will fill prisons with criminals who are **far less** dangerous than murderers.
その新しい犯罪防止法は、殺人犯よりもずっと危険性の少ない犯罪者たちで刑務所をいっぱいにするであろう。

150. **Both Jimmy and Eric, as well as Jeff**, intended to be famous.
ジェフ同様ジミーとエリックも有名になるつもりだった。

151. The lawyer reached his conclusion **on the basis of** a rumor that his client had been forced to pretend that she had indeed hired a private detective for some reason.
弁護士が結論を下したのは、何らかの理由で私立探偵を確かに雇ったというふりをするよう、彼の依頼人が強要されていたという噂に基づいてであった。

152. Miss White has been known to give wake-up calls to students who are chronically late to school so that they get up and get there **on time**.
ホワイト先生は、いつも遅刻する生徒たちにモーニング・コールをかけて彼らを起こし、時間通りに登校させることで知られている。

153. Dozens of old books are stacked on top of **one another** on his desk.
何十冊もの古い本が、彼の机の上に積み重なっている。

154. **One in three flights** last year was cancelled, delayed, or diverted to another airport; 173 million passengers were affected.
昨年、3便に1便はキャンセルされたか、遅れたか、あるいは目的地以外の空港に変更され、1.73億人の乗客に影響が出た。

155. The school that the juvenile delinquent had been sent to was **one of** 13 reform schools that received children from the D.C. area.
その不良が送られた学校は、ワシントン地区から子供を受け入れる13の少年院の1つであった。

156. This is a neighborhood that basically deals with **its own** problems internally.
ここは、自らの問題は基本的に内部で対処する地域である。

157. The international student advisor made **only a few** exceptions to the rules regarding transferring credits from foreign universities.
インターナショナル・スチューデント・アドバイザーは、外国大学からの単位振り替えに関する規則にごくわずかの例外しか認めなかった。

158. The father came **out of** retirement to assist his son, who had taken over his business.
父親は、すでに仕事を継いでいた息子を助けるために、隠居生活から復帰した。

159. The teachers are trying very hard to **persuade their least-motivated students that learning is fun**.
教員たちは、学ぶことが楽しいことを最もやる気のない生徒たちに一生懸命悟らせる努力をしている。

160. The detective feared that his client might be **planning to flee** the scene with the crime's only witness.
探偵は、依頼者がその犯罪の唯一の目撃者とともに現場を逃げるつもりなのかもしれないと危惧した。

161. **Like physicists**, theoretical linguists look for principles in human language.
物理学者と同様に、理論言語学者も人間言語内に原理を追い求める。

162. This letter is not interesting because there is **little news**.
この手紙は、ほとんどニュースがないのでおもしろくない。

163. For the hospital sequence, the movie director chose the Fairfield Hills Hospital, a facility **located in** Newtown, Connecticut.
その映画監督は、病院の場面を撮るのにコネチカット州ニュータウンにある病院、フェアフィールド・ヒルズ病院を選んだ。

164. This gorgeous spring is **making up for** the very cold winter.
今年のすばらしい春は、とても寒かった冬の埋め合わせになっている。

165. Dorothy is a very attractive woman with a wonderful sense of humor, and there is something about her that **makes you believe** that she must be heaven-sent.
ドロシーはすばらしいユーモアのセンスを持った、とても魅力的な女性で、彼女には天与の人に違いないと思わせる何かがある。

166. There are **many** free language **programs** on radio and TV in Japan.
日本には、ラジオとテレビの無料言語講座がたくさんある。

167. Although Takeo wanted to study in Indonesia, he didn't have **much information** about the country.
タケオはインドネシアで勉強したかったが、その国について多くの情報を持ち合わせていなかった。

168. Farmers' children may **no longer** be able to study at the institute because of the high tuition.
農民の子供は、授業料が高いので、もはやその学校で学ぶことはできないかもしれない。

169. Child development experts suggest you play music for your child **not** for the purpose of building brain cells **but** for entertainment.
幼児育成の専門家は、脳細胞を発達させる目的のためではなく、娯楽のために子供に音楽をかけてやるべきだと勧める。

170. One of the best reasons for taking this whiskey tasting class is that learning in a bar is **not only** expensive **but also** difficult.
このウィスキーの聞き酒クラスを取るべきもっともな理由の1つは、バーで学ぶのには金がかかるばかりでなく、難しいということである。

171. The mother wanted to attribute her child's bad mood to a lack of sleep **rather than** to his moody disposition.
母親は、我が子の不機嫌を彼の気分屋の性格というよりも睡眠不足のせいにしたがった。

172. Those laws **regarding** sanitation are very unpopular with janitors.
公衆衛生についてのその法律は、管理人たちにはとても不評である。

173. I think our company should **relocate to** a new city.
我々の会社は、新しい都市に移転するべきだと思う。

174. The principal said she would allow class representatives to **serve** as advisers to the faculty meeting.
校長は、学級委員たちが職員会議の顧問になることを許すと言った。

175. Even the nearest hospital is **several miles** away.
一番近い病院でさえ、数マイル離れている。

176. Mr. May's lesson was something that **should have been** remembered by all his followers.
メイ氏の教訓は、彼の信奉者みんなが覚えておくべきだった。

177. The attorney general's recent comments about dealing with gun violence did not **show promise** of a good beginning for the administration on this issue.
拳銃暴力の対処に関する司法長官の最近のコメントは、政府にとってこの問題に関するよいスタートを予見するものではなかった。

178. The problems of urban schools in the U.S. are **so great that** they require firm decisions by people with financial and political clout.
アメリカにおける都会の学校の問題はとてもひどいので、財政的そして政治的影響力を持つ人々によるしっかりした決断が必要である。

179. In 1995, the guitar company altered its logo **so that** "Ray Vaughn" would appear in larger letters.
1995年にそのギター会社は、「レイ・ボーン」の文字がより大きく表示されるように会社のロゴを変えた。

180. The professor let us **spend time** in his office in order to get to know us better.
教授は、我々のことをよりよく知ろうと、彼の研究室を使わせてくれた。

181. We expect the building to be finished within **the next two weeks**.
その建物は、ここ２週間以内に完成するだろうと我々は思っている。

182. The timid speaker was intimidated by the thousands of faces in the crowd.
臆病な演説者は、何千もの聴衆の顔を見ておびえてしまった。

183. An unidentified source said the civilians at the controls were under close supervision, and their presence was **unrelated to** the accident.
未確認筋によると、操縦していた一般人たちは厳重な監督下にあり、彼らの存在は事故とは無縁だということであった。

184. The detective drove **up the long, expansive driveway** to the Mercury mansion.
探偵の車は、マーキュリー大邸宅の長く、広々した車道を登っていった。

185. The actress had to **get used to running** around in very high, spiked heels.
女優は、先細のとても高いヒール靴を履いて走り回るのに慣れなければならなかった。

186. Humility may be more **useful for** us in addressing the question of how to prevent misuse of genetic information as it becomes more available.
遺伝情報が得られるにつれ、その誤用をいかに防ぐかという問題に対処するのに、謙虚さが我々にとってより有用になるのかも知れない。

187. Mario **wishes** that he **had** enough time to complete his homework before 3 o'clock.
マリオは、もっと時間があって３時前に宿題を終わらせられたらなあ、と思っている。

188. Acting is like dancing **with** someone who is a really good dancer.
演技とは、本当にダンスのうまい人と踊るようなものである。

189. I **would rather transfer** to another school than attend that stupid class.
あの馬鹿らしい授業に出るよりも転校したほうがましだ。

190. I love shopping; I **would rather** that stores **stayed** open until midnight.
私はショッピングに目がない。午前０時まで店が開いていてほしいのだが。

191. If you want a statistical report on universities in the U.S., you should look for special editions of magazines **such as** Newsweek and U.S. News and World Report.
アメリカの大学に関する統計的レポートがほしいなら、ニューズウィークおよびU.S.ニュース・アンド・ワールド・レポートのような雑誌の特集号を探すとよい。

192. The fact that one woman's passion could have **such** a positive effect as this on so many people around her is amazing.
１人の女性の情熱が、周りにいるとても多くの人にこのようなポジティブな影響を与えられたとは驚きだ。

193. **In response** to written questions from the committee this week, an attorney for Candy Loving indicated she had given an "enormous sum of money" to her lover's library.
委員会から今週寄せられた書面による質問に応じて、キャンディ・ラビングの弁護士は、彼女が愛人の図書館に「多額の金銭」を寄付していたことを明らかにした。

194. It is often said that the musician Clive Davis has **such a big ego that** he thinks CD's were named after him.
よく言われることだが、ミュージシャンであるクライブ・デイビスはうぬぼれがとても強く、CDは自分の名にちなんでつけられたと思っている。

195. We have **taken** special **care** to see that the new toy will contain no dangerous parts.
その新しいおもちゃに危険な部品が使われないよう、我々は特別な注意を払った。

196. I was completely **taken by surprise** when the supervisor came to observe my class.
スーパバイザーが私の授業を見に来たとき、私は完全に不意をつかれた。

197. No matter how **beautiful** my cake **looks**, it has to taste good, or I'm not a good pastry cook.
私のケーキがどんなに美しく見えても、おいしくなければならない。でないと、私はよい菓子職人でないことになる。

198. Concerned parties complained **that** this horror film should not have been made available to minors, even if accompanied by their parents.
このホラー映画は、たとえ親の同伴があったとしても、子供たちには公開されるべきではなかったと、懸念のぬぐえない人たちは不平を述べた。

199. **The development** of a new teaching method requires much research.
新しい教授法の開発には、多くの研究が必要だ。

200. **The higher** up we go, **the colder** it becomes.
高く行けば行くほど、寒くなる。